The Story Behind..

I Love You, Mum –
I Promise I Won't Die

Edited by Mark Wheeller

Salamander Street

Published in 2022 by Salamander Street Ltd,
272 Bath Street, Glasgow, G2 4JR (info@salamanderstreet.com).

© Mark Wheeller/DSMF/Annette Hulme, 2022

Photography © Chris Webb Photography (p. 46), Tara Hook (p. 55), Spargo-Mabbs family (p. 79)

PB ISBN: 9781914228766

10 9 8 7 6 5 4 3 2 1

Further copies of this publication can be purchased from
www.salamanderstreet.com

Acknowledgements

Fiona Spargo-Mabbs and family for their friendship, inspiration and trust in us (Oasis Youth Theatre) as an unknown company.

The development team from Oasis Youth Theatre 2015-2016 for their work on the original production of *I Love You Mum – I Promise I Won't Die*: Karmin Arnold; James Bratby; Sally Britton; Haydn Carrington; Kat Chivers: George Davies; Lewis Evans; Chelsea Fisher; Jodie Fisher; Tim Ford; Conner Handstock; Paul Ibbott; Richard Long; Emily Moulsdale; Alysha-Jade Patis; Anna Pego; Olivia Prendergast; Natascha Thomas; Matt Savage; Carley Sefton-Wilson; Amy Sturrock; Danny Sturrock; Matthew Sturrock; Boston Sutton; Joe Tucker; Callum Watts; Chris Webb; Ollie Webb.

The Daniel Spargo-Mabbs Foundation for their vision, emotional and financial support to both the OYT and professional productions.

Izzy Forrester, Dan's drama teacher, for having the idea to approach me to write a play that told his story, for her confidence that mine would be a safe pair of hands to entrust it to.

Dan's friends, and his (then) girlfriend Jenna and her family, for their trust and generosity in sharing such rich memories, insights, pain and joy, for the sake of their friend Dan, and for other young people who'll come to experience his story.

All named in the book for their recollections specifically written in response to my questionnaire.

Annette Hulme for her expertise in creating the scheme of work.

Rachel Wheeller, who supports my personal and working life so whole-heartedly.

Roy Nevitt and Stantonbury Campus Theatre for introducing me to documentary theatre and a general theatre education.

Various newspaper reviewers/adjudicators who have allowed more people to hear about my plays.

Danny Sturrock for his unique support and friendship throughout my OYT years. Not only did he help with technical aspects of this production but he was also a powerhouse behind the Wheellerplays digital presence which continues into the future.

Sophie Gorell Barnes and all at MBA Literary Agency for continued belief.

StopWatch, Wizard and Tie It Up Theatre Companies for their professional productions of this play.

Dawn Boyfield, Evie Efthimiou and Lynda Taylor from dbda (later Zinc Publishing) who put their trust in Wheellerplays and set so many balls rolling.

Bloomsbury for publishing I Love You, Mum – I Promise I Won't Die under their Methuen 'plays for young people' banner.

George Spender for rescuing Wheellerplays in the 2020 pandemic and for working so closely with me to make so much of my work available more widely.

Photographs/Images Cover: Salamander Street

Note: Every effort has been made to acknowledge and credit the originators and copyright holders of the images used within this book.

Contents

Foreword: Daniel Spargo-Mabbs

ORIGINALLY WRITTEN FOR HIS MEMORIAL SERVICE
BY IZZY FORRESTER, DAN'S DRAMA TEACHER

I will miss Dan so much. To be honest, I can't really believe he's gone, that I'll never hear his voice again. All the pictures I've seen over the last few days have reminded me exactly what he was like: lovely, maddening, clever, terribly rude, talented, deeply inappropriate at times! – but above all, immensely lovable.

My abiding memory of him, which lots of his year group will remember, is how he used to try to give me a bear hug whenever he saw me, to the point where I would beg Alice or Hope or Jack or anyone really – to keep him away from me! But they would usually be laughing so hard that they were no help at all! And I remember how he would always knock on my window on his way past and pull a face at me to make me laugh.

In Drama GCSE, there are so many memories of him: the deep love he had for dressing up in the most inappropriate costumes he could find, the time he was reading 'The Hobbit' aloud to Toby and they were just in a world of their own, how he used to tease all the girls and (I apologise for the rudeness) pass wind whenever and wherever he could – all with a great big gleeful smile on his face! But most gratifying for me was how much his confidence increased as the two years went by – how amazed he was when the girls all wanted to work with him in the performance exam, because he was so talented and a really amazing actor. He had so much potential.

But for all his exuberance, he could be terribly under confident and frightened. When I gave him a lead role in Joseph, he was so proud to be cast but equally terrified of singing and acting solo. I can clearly remember him telling me that he couldn't do it, that he would be rubbish and that I should cast someone else because anyone would be better than him! It took me quite a while to rehearse with him, and persuade him that he could do it, and would be amazing, and…he was!

In the Shakespeare evening, when he played Macbeth, despite a terrible sore throat, he was so compelling. This morning, I was looking at the recording of the evening, and in the bottom right of the screen, you can see Fiona and Tim, Dan's parents, watching him with such pride and love. Then, at the end of the evening, the cast come back in, and you can see Dan make straight for his parents and give Fiona a huge hug. It's a truly moving moment.

I know that we will all miss Dan so much. Remember Dan in your hearts. Remember how much we all loved him. And whenever you remember him, do it with a smile.

Preface

OYT – 2015 CONTEXT

I remember sitting with my Oasis Youth Theatre (OYT) group early on in the development of *I Love You, Mum – I Promise I Won't Die* (*ILYMIPIWD*) and saying, "Wouldn't it be amazing if this play we're embarking on became a set text? It is possible. We know that now. Those who worked with me to develop *Hard to Swallow* or *Missing Dan Nolan* could never have conceived of that possibility. People may go on to study this, and (will have to) be interested in how we did what we did. So, remember these rehearsals. I may not be here to tell this story, and you may be asked about it all at some point in the distant future!"

Never could any of us have imagined this would happen within seven years of that meeting in May 2015, just as two of my previous plays had been announced as GCSE Drama set texts for the (then) new Eduqas and OCR GCSE Drama 9-1 examinations. (And I am very much still here!) For my part, I'm thrilled to be writing a book about a play where, for the first time in any of those I've been asked to write about, I had a team of experienced adults contributing to the production, rather than me operating as a one-man band alongside a few enthusiastic, older students. Our inexperience back in the days of *Hard to Swallow* was inspiring, but it proved difficult to offer much credibility for 'study' of our process, which was largely, "Let's try this and see how it works". For *ILYMIPIWD*, thought went into each of the technical components, with different people taking on separate responsibilities. Each has their own story, which, using an oral history technique, I will bring together in one volume, alongside recollections of the cast and those who contributed their words and memories to make the script itself.

By 2015 verbatim theatre had come of age. I had been on a 'serious' playwriting course (2007-2008, run by John Burgess at the Southampton Nuffield theatre) and, to my surprise and delight, writing a play based on personal testimony was a component. In 2011, Alecky Blythe's verbatim musical, *London Road*, presented at the National Theatre, achieved huge critical acclaim, and brought the term 'verbatim' to my attention. Suddenly, what I had been doing since the early 1980s was in vogue, rather than looked down on by those who influenced opinion in the theatre world.

OYT was riding the crest of a wave in 2012. We had celebrated the 25th anniversary of *Too Much Punch For Judy* with a production that brought us significant attention. From that point on, schools attended our productions from far afield to see 'how we did it', using our performances for inspiration and review purposes in their GCSE exams. This offered a boost to our ticket sales, leading to specially organised school performances.

For years OYT had entered the All England Theatre Festival (AETF), never progressing beyond the first round. However, three productions we had entered between 2008 and 2014 (*Race To Be Seen*, *One Million To Stop The Traffik* & *Jack*) won through to the prestigious English Final. OYT was being noticed, and our belief that we were doing something special was being affirmed.

DVDs of our OYT productions were released by my publisher (at that time), Ten Alps/Zinc Publishing. The *Punch* DVD was particularly impressive, not only the production but also the videography, by our unusually talented technician, Danny Sturrock. We were so fortunate to have him to document our work. This, together with the advent of Facebook, where drama teacher groups sang the praises of my work in a way that mainstream theatre never had done, put my plays in front of a wider audience.

On a personal level, my TIE touring productions (*Too Much Punch*, *Hard to Swallow*, *Chicken*, *Legal Weapon*, *Arson About*, *The Gate Escape* and *Missing Dan Nolan*) continued to solidify my reputation over a sustained period. These also led to invitations to run workshops across the world, and professional playwriting commissions. In the year before *ILYMIPIWD* I had accepted two.

The first was from (and with) Voices of the Holocaust, to tell the story of Susan Pollack MBE, a Holocaust survivor. *Kindness – A Legacy of the Holocaust* has now become a high quality touring TIE production, and illustrated a unique way of enabling the words of those affected to be heard without them having to be available in person to do so. This was a high profile and prestigious commission to land, thanks to Voices Artistic Director, Cate Hollis.

The second came from the Victoria Shanghai Academy (VSA), an international school in Hong Kong, who I'd made contact with on a workshop I'd run in Hong Kong. They wanted me to develop a verbatim play of my choice. I chose to tell the explosive and dramatic tale of Chris Gilfoy, World Champion Banger Racer. I had taught Chris in the early 1990s. He had offered (via his improvisations) words for my second most popular play, *Chicken!*. When VSA came to perform the resultant play, *Chequered Flags to Chequered Futures*, they made a surreal offer: to bring a cast from OYT to Hong Kong, at their expense, along with Chris and his family, to perform *Chicken!* as part of a double bill of Wheellerplays performances.

Lewis Evans (Jack in the original OYT production – Year 11 at the start): I vividly remember Mark asking me if I wanted to go to Hong Kong, taking me to one side before a *Silas Marner* rehearsal, saying something like, "I don't know whether this will happen… I think it will, but not for a while, but…would you want to come to Hong Kong, if we can get a production of *Chicken* together fast?" I remember responding with a very blunt and shocked, "Fuck off! Seriously?". Then, "Can Ross come?". I was overwhelmed that this new hobby could potentially take me to the other side of the world!

From the moment the trip was confirmed, to rehearsing *Chicken*, getting on the plane, exploring Hong Kong, performing the shows, it was an experience I will never forget. The show completely outshone my birthday, to the point I forgot it, until everyone in the audience sang 'Happy Birthday' to me! We became young, foreign celebrities for a week!

As a result of this trip, my attitude changed towards my career choice. I was thinking, "If I can go to Hong Kong doing this at the age of 14, imagine where this might take me for the rest of my life!". After that, within OYT, people looked to us when things got difficult, or needed inspiration, even the older ones! It was a turning point.

I remember a brief conversation with Mark in Hong Kong about this new play he was writing. He gave the impression it would be something 'big'. When it was announced, I remember thinking to myself, "Yep, I'm in!". There was a lot more interest in being part of this new production from people outside our school. I've never really thought about why that was. Maybe the success of previous productions, or perhaps people wanted something different to musical theatre, which was the norm for youth productions in our area. The original cast was around 30-35, but it soon whittled down. I always knew I'd be there until the very end… and I was! Now look where the production is!

Lewis mentions that this production attracted people from further afield, which supports my impression that OYT was picking up a reputation for its work, but I had forgotten how this affected its membership. However, only two cast members that had no direct affiliation to Oasis Academy (who funded my role as OYT director) survived the eighteen-month development period. Perhaps these 'outsiders' weren't aware of how committed we were when they signed up, whereas those who knew me from school would have known only too well!

Lewis went on to fulfil a second prophesy I made in the same conversation quoted above. "I won't be surprised if someone here goes on to perform in a professional production of this play. It happened in *Too Much Punch For Judy, Chicken, Legal Weapon* and *Arson About…* so it's a reasonable possibility".

Lewis not only performed in the original OYT production and video as (most notably) Jack, but he recreated that role (amongst others) for the professional StopWatch Theatre Company tour. He now runs his own theatre company, Box House, and at the time of writing, is looking to adopt the rights to tour *Game Over*.

Everything I have spoken of here raised my self-confidence. I saw myself as a successful playwright, as well as a successful drama teacher/youth theatre director. The *ILYMIPIWD* production started as an acorn in our Academy Youth Theatre but grew into a fully rooted tree. The script was published by (Bloomsbury) Methuen Drama, the first time I had been published by them. The commissioning editor studied *Hard to Swallow* at school so was aware of my work.

The play has toured professionally in the UK every year since it was published and, in its short life, has already amassed over 500 licensed performances. During the Covid-19 pandemic a film was made of the Tie It Up Theatre professional production, which provides a permanent, high-quality testament to the work of the Daniel Spargo-Mabbs Foundation (DSMF). Plans are already in place for the Octopus Dream Theatre Company, in association with the York Theatre Royal, to tour the full play into Studio venues across the country in 2023.

The *ILYMIPIWD* story is an incredible one, and I am delighted to share how it came to be. Strange though… when it was originally commissioned, it was never the intention for my OYT to premiere it.

Chapter 1

A PLAY?

Fiona Spargo-Mabbs (Daniel Spargo-Mabbs' mum): The story of the play coming into existence began with a Spanish playwright, who contacted us a couple of months after Dan died, via the charity website. He'd read about Dan – the media channels got Dan's story all over the place – and he wanted to write a play about him. This was so unexpected, and so bizarre, but the world had turned totally upside down since the moment Dan died, and nothing made any sense any more, and this was just part of the general madness. We agreed to meet him for coffee when he passed through London in a few weeks' time. It turned out he'd already started writing the play. He'd got Dan as a moody teenager, rowing with Tim, hiding away in his room – not what Dan was like at all, nor Tim. He wanted to speak to Dan's friends, to Jacob, to Jenna, to the police, the paramedics, the consultant. I felt uneasy about the whole thing and held off, but he kept emailing, and pushing me. I felt it was getting totally out of control, but I was still in such a vulnerable place that I didn't know how to make it stop. I'd arranged to have coffee with Izzy Forrester (Dan's drama teacher) for the first time since Dan died – we'd only met at parents' evenings and school productions, and then Dan's funeral, but I felt very fond of her because Dan did, and I knew she loved Dan, and she was to become one of the DSM Foundation's first trustees. I told her about the Spanish playwright and how out of hand it was becoming, she asked for his email address, said she'd deal with it, and I never heard from him again. You don't mess with Ms Forrester!

I am shocked by treatment of any life story that a) doesn't choose to enlist the support of that person before you begin, and b) doesn't treat the facts as sacrosanct. I never want a disclaimer about straying from the truth of a dramatic version of a real event; that's an important premise for me. At the time of writing, there's a high profile case of a new Disney film/mini-series ('Pistol') which apparently failed to get permission from the Sex Pistols' lead singer, Johnny Rotten, before embarking on the film. People should have a right over their life stories, more than the rights a playwright has over their plays! For me, this is a question of what's right... and in this instance my stance on these ethics helped me to 'land the job'.

Izzy Forrester (Dan's drama teacher): Fiona and Tim were very clear from early on; they wanted to educate young people on the dangers of drugs, and empower them to make safer choices. Drama is such a powerful tool to engage pupils, and allows conversations and change. As a Drama teacher with many years' experience, I had seen this in action, including directing a performance of *Legal Weapon* in my second year at Archbishop Tenison's. I'd studied some of Mark's other plays with GCSE classes, including Dan's class (*Legal Weapon*). I was considering the best time to talk to Fiona and Tim, but the conversation naturally came up, and I agreed to contact Mark and be involved in the whole process, as much as needed… if it happened at all. Fiona is an educator herself, so was positive about the potential power of a TIE play. I was humbled in her faith in me that it would be good!

Fiona Spargo-Mabbs: Izzy suggested we really should think about using drama as part of what we did as a drug education charity. She said there's a playwright, Mark Wheeller, (who I'd never heard of), who writes incredible plays for young people about issues that affect them, and she thought he'd be perfect for Dan's story. Would we mind if she contacted him via his website? We didn't mind at all, so she did, and so it all began. There was a huge amount of trust I needed to find though, in Mark and the process and all that might follow. It was incredibly scary. It felt like handing Dan over for public consumption, and once I'd let go, I'd have no idea who'd make what of him, or what had happened to him. I needed to know he'd be taken great care of if I did entrust him to someone else, especially if they'd then be passing him on to who knows who else.

Jacob Spargo-Mabbs (Dan's older brother): The idea of turning the experience into a play hadn't come from those of us who knew Dan, but it planted the idea. For me, the experience was still very raw. Dan hadn't been dead for long. It seemed grotesque to me to go to any lengths to try to relive or recreate that in any way. I was still very much in shock, and it was hard for me to see beyond how traumatising the experience was. However, talking to Mark, and friends and family, made me see the value of a play to convey the message that the Foundation wanted to share. Mark clearly didn't want to sensationalise – he seemed genuinely committed to theatre as a form of education.

Tim Spargo-Mabbs: We didn't want a misleading account to get into circulation but Izzy, Dan's drama teacher, was serious about the potential the story had for drama.

Izzy Forrester: So I emailed Mark, and asked whether he might be interested in writing a play.

Sat, 3 May 2014, 21:20

Dear Mark

In January of this year, we lost one of our students as a result of taking MDMA. He was an amazing actor and just a fantastic young man; his loss has been devastating. I am writing to you on behalf of his amazing parents. You may have seen Dan's story in the press; there has been a lot of coverage and his parents have done interviews on radio and TV to try to save other young lives. I am in awe of their strength and bravery.

Tim and Fiona have set up the Daniel Spargo-Mabbs Foundation (http://www. dsmfoundation.org.uk) to try to prevent other deaths. Part of their website says: "Dan's death was a tragedy that needn't have happened. He thought he'd be safe trying a tiny amount of a drug just once. But Dan wasn't safe; no-one's safe. Dan's story isn't unique. But if we can save just one more tragedy like this, if we can prevent another family going through the pain of losing a child, Dan's death will have more meaning".

I have taught your plays to my students several times (most recently your updated Legal Weapon II*) and am a great admirer of your work. So, when Fiona and Tim were talking about the idea of using drama to promote their message, I immediately thought of you, discussed it with them, and they asked me to contact you.*

Dan was such an original, compassionate, and just a hilarious young man; he was hugely popular with his friends, beloved for his humour (often very saucy!) and his loyalty. I think that one of your plays would be an amazing tool to spread the message, and just a great work.

I really hope you will consider this idea, and I look forward very much to hearing from you.

With best wishes

Izzy Forrester

Chapter 2

THE COMMISSION

I have always been passionate about raising awareness of drug misuse, not because I have had an awful experience myself, but because a TV programme, *Gail Is Dead*, still available on YouTube, was shown to me as a 4th Year at school (Year 10 in current-speak). The forceful impact of this programme inspired me, not only to avoid experimenting with drugs myself, but also started my belief that presentations to school students do have a powerful impact and can (not will) change behaviour. The reason I hadn't developed a play about drug misuse, despite actually wanting to do so, was:

a) I'd never had the opportunity or courage to approach anyone who had suffered a loss to make it happen. I had considered it when the Leah Betts situation was in the news, but lacked the courage to make an unsolicited request.

and

b) my friend, Danny Sturrock, had written a drug awareness play in 2001, *Gagging For It*, which was proving successful, and I didn't want to step on his success.

When Izzy's email arrived out of the blue in my inbox, I spoke to Danny. He agreed that this, as a verbatim play, would be substantially different from his, and that I should allow discussions to progress.

> **Izzy Forrester**: I was delighted when Mark responded really quickly and so positively. It seemed like a sign that this would be a good way to support the newly formed Daniel Spargo-Mabbs Foundation, and it has certainly turned out to be.

4 May 2014, 15:03

Hi Izzy,

Thanks so much for making contact with me re this. Potentially VERY exciting! I would LOVE to be involved! It seems like the 'story' has a head start with the coverage achieved so far.

The problem will be that I will need paying. Best cut to the chase straight away. This would normally mean going via my agent, but I can short-circuit all of this by letting you know that the most recent play cost £4,500. That gives you an idea…and may make you want to stop reading any further and tell me to go away! (I hope not). The Foundation would retain some rights… this is where the agent will come in… I would imagine (ONLY 'I would imagine') about £25% of any income the play may generate through script sales, public performances etc. It's never a huge amount unless it goes on to be HUGELY successful and adapts for TV, etc, but who knows? An advantage of asking me is that generally my plays do get published. Once published, teachers will be interested to at least have a look… and then hopefully use.

I think with this subject matter it would be a great fit. I have not done a play on this subject previously. I would want to do it as a verbatim play, telling the true story so, will need the family and friends to be prepared to speak.

I have a Youth Theatre… so there is a possibility that they could put it on… or perhaps you could do the premiere… that might be better. I have contact with a few professional groups who have toured my work. They are always interested in looking at new work I do but there are huge costs, and you'd need proper sponsorship in place to make this happen… but if the play exists it means it can happen. If not, it can't!

I am currently about to start on a commission (Holocaust) for the Voices company. This should be completed by October. I am retiring from teaching in Aug 2015 so will have more availability to do stuff after that, which should tie in magnificently!

If none of this has put you off, please let's talk. My home phone number is xxxxx xxxxxx. I am around tomorrow and much of Tuesday and Thursday daytimes. Let me know if you think there is some mileage in this.

Once again, thanks for considering me with this idea.

Mark

5 May 2014, 10:02

Good morning Mark

Having talked to Fiona, she and Tim are really happy, and moved, that you would like to be involved, and have asked me to say they would definitely be interested in going ahead. They need to talk to the Trustees of the Foundation about the cost, and when they have done so, I will get back to you. I feel pretty sure that they will agree.

Thanks again so much, Mark, and I will contact you again when we have a decision, which should be very soon.

Izzy

5 May 2014, 10:52

Izzy that is simply INCREDIBLE... thanks very much for what is an exciting start to my Bank Holiday... tho I shall try not to count my chickens.

I will work with Fiona and Tim all the way, and they will retain editorial control. They will have that anyway, as, if I'm using their words, they will choose what they do and don't tell me.

One question is presumably, was Dan was with other friends that night? How will they feel about this going ahead?

Very keen to chat and hear the thoughts of the trustees.

Thanks so much. I hope you are having as good a bank holiday!!!

Mark

5 May 2014, 20:28

Hi Mark.

I can't tell you how great it is that you are so keen – it means the world to Fiona and Tim.

As far as I know, none of his friends are implicated, although there are a lot of feelings of guilt. Two young men were arrested for selling Dan the drug.

Fiona and I are talking about potential fundraising ideas, particularly involving our school. I'll be in touch again very soon.

Best wishes

Izzy

Mon, 5 May 2014, 21:01

Hi Izzy,

Fab news… yes, I am a bit of an enthusiast… just want to drop everything and come and meet you all and do the interviews!

Do keep me in touch with developments as and when. Thanks.

Mark

11 May 2014, 22:50

Hi Mark

Sorry it's such a late reply; it's been a mad weekend – you know what exam and coursework deadline season is like in Drama!

Anyway, Fiona and I met yesterday and had a long talk. The happy result is that the Trustees agree that the play is a very exciting and worthwhile venture, and we have plans in place for fundraising to cover the cost.

We discussed contact with you, and starting the process, and whilst I was concerned about how Fiona would feel, she is determined to get started. I know that you will be very sensitive, and you will love Fiona and Tim. They are very special people.

I have told Fiona that I am more than happy to be involved in the project, and will help however I can.

With very best wishes,

Izzy

12 May 2014, 13:47

Hi Fiona,

I am so pleased you are willing to trust me with your family's story. I think the title might already be there… in that Daily Mail *headline…* I Love You, Mum – I Promise I Won't Die. *I know it's long but I think it say everything. We can chat about it but I really like it.*

I would like to chat to you and see how (and when) we can start to progress things. I think it will be better to speak rather than prolonged emails at first.

I look forward to hearing from you.

Mark

> **Fiona Spargo-Mabbs:** Mark and I spoke on the phone a lot before we first met, and that really helped develop a sense of reassurance – that we'd be very involved in everything, that we'd be able to say if something wasn't right or how we wanted it, that it mattered to him to understand Dan, and us, and what happened, and to communicate that in a way we were comfortable with (as far as that could be possible) and that aligned with the message we wanted young people to receive, which was what had motivated all of this from the beginning. From the moment Dan died, we'd wanted to do everything we could to stop any harm happening to anyone else. This play became an integral part of that.

> **Tim Spargo-Mabbs:** I had the sense, knowing nothing about modern drama, of this being like a door that we were invited to walk through, knowing nothing of whether it would succeed or fail, or where it might lead. Like so many things in the timeline since Dan's death, it seemed like I needed to take this chance, as I would always wonder what would have happened if I didn't. Like so many of those things, it was the gateway to a new part of my life, and to an increase in the ways of making Dan's story known. I am overwhelmingly glad that we pushed on this door, and that it opened the way it did.

I had already faced criticism about *Too Much Punch for Judy* and, the original *One Million to Stop the Traffik* (2010), being too 'finger-wagging'. Although I still think this is the right approach for the topics of those plays, the issues surrounding drug education were more nuanced. Unbeknownst to me, I was to meet a family for whom avoiding a didactic approach was an equally important goal.

Chapter 3

INTERVIEWS

I remember the convivial phone conversations with Fiona, which led to an early sense of 'friendship'. We both imagined the play that emerged would be premiered at Dan's school, Archbishop Tenison's, and directed by Izzy. I was writing it for them to perform and then, perhaps, I might put a production on but, as I was retiring it seemed unlikely. I remember feeling what an opportunity this would have been for OYT but did not think it was appropriate to mention my private thoughts (and disappointment) to anyone. To make matters worse for me, I was struggling to decide what I could work on for OYTs next production that would grab their (OYT's) attention in a way I knew Dan's story would achieve.

Fiona Spargo-Mabbs: I'd built a sense that Mark could be trusted, but I felt very responsible for Dan's friends, having asked them to share their own stories, when it was all so raw, and they were still so very vulnerable. I hoped what we were asking wasn't something totally unthinkable, or ridiculously insensitive. It was such an extraordinary situation I had no benchmark to judge whether asking them to do this was pressuring (would they feel they had to for Dan's sake/because others were?), or manipulative (would they feel they had to because they wouldn't want to hurt us or let us down?). They were trusting us, as were their parents, and we were trusting Mark in turn.

I travelled up to Croydon, excited for the first set of interviews and arrived to the warmest possible reception, with a family who already felt like friends. We relaxed together over a meal (salad and pizza) which is something I'd never experienced at any interview session I'd been involved in. It offered a perfect start, allowing the ice to be broken gently.

The interviews had been organised for two days separated by a few weeks. On the first I was timetabled to chat with Jenna, Dan's girlfriend at the time of his death. Her mum, Kate, came to support her, and ended up contributing to such an extent that I asked if I could include her words as well! She was taken by surprise, but after some thought agreed. I'm so glad she was there. Her memories from another parent's perspective added so much to the final play, and of course I would never have known what her involvement was to consider inviting her to be involved!

The interviews with Dan's friends were a few weeks later, but one friend, Hope, was on holiday then, so she popped in during the afternoon and lit the room up with her effervescence and poignant memories. This explains why Fiona appears in the first part of the play ('ILYM') alongside Hope in what is the friends story. Fiona was there, and chipped in to help Hope tell her truth. Again, this was no planned thing, just a decision based on Hope's availability.

Hope: Dan was my first boyfriend, then my best friend at school from 13-16. I put myself forward to be interviewed because I wanted to make sure that what happened to Dan didn't happen in vain. It was awful to feel so helpless afterwards, but if what we went through can make young people think twice about dealing or taking drugs that they're not sure of, then it has been worth speaking up. I remember feeling very isolated after Dan's death. There was a divide between his various friends so. being able to do the interview on my own was special as I didn't feel I needed to hide how I really felt. I just sat and talked about our friendship without any judgement.

Jacob Spargo-Mabbs: I was living with my parents after coming home from university for the summer. Mark had a tape recorder and explained how he would record straight to tape and then transcribe later, and joked about using old technology. I don't remember what I said, but he made me feel at ease (as much as a person could feel at ease when talking about the recent death of their sibling), and he demonstrated that his aim was to create a useful educational tool.

Tim: I remember being fascinated by Mark's use of cassettes, very much a part of my childhood/adolescence. I remember being asked searching questions, and reaching deep within myself to access feelings and images that I did not previously know to be there. I remain very grateful for this, as the words appear to have stood up over the intervening years.

Researching a play such is this placed me in a unique position where all barriers are dismantled. I was able to ask literally anything for the good of the project. This led to instantly open conversations. I was aware this feeling was not mutual, as I wasn't talking about my life nearly so openly!

Fiona: The interviews were in some sense just what I was doing all the time – talking about Dan, reliving and reworking every moment before, during and after he died. I found it hard not to talk about Dan at any and every opportunity, and the interviews happened just six months later when my head was still so hard at work processing and trying to make sense of this senseless thing. It was always a gift to be able to talk about Dan, and especially to someone who was so very interested in it all, which Mark really was. He asked very pertinent and probing questions, which made me look at some things in a different way, and think about things I hadn't before, and revisit places that had been too painful to fall back into. Some of this was harrowing, and I remember, after he left that first time, I sat in the garden in the dark for hours, crying.

Poor Fiona! I was driving back to Southampton excited and couldn't wait to conduct the interviews with Dan's other friends, followed by even more probing interviews with Fiona, Tim and Jacob. I remember being so frustrated that OYT were not able to premiere the play, as the production would go out of my control. I wondered… could I offer to do a performance in Southampton at the same time as the Tenison's production? I didn't know how to ask without seeming pushy. In between the two interview sessions I started to transcribe the testimony I'd recorded – a long, time-consuming job, but I became more familiar with the words.

Two weeks later I was on my way up to Croydon again… this time to a room at the back of a church, with Izzy and a number of Dan's closest friends.

Izzy Forrester: When I talked to Dan's friends at school about the play, they were thoughtful in their responses, but agreed that it would be a good idea. Lots of them had studied Drama with me and were particularly pleased that it was with Mark. There were only three who were hesitant to take part, including two who, it would later come to light, were much more complicit than they had led us all to believe and one who just did not reply at all and was subsequently interviewed by the police about his involvement.

I don't know where I got this idea from because it's not expressed in much of what anyone said to me, but I sensed some wariness from them about the project. I remember someone saying, "We would understand if it were a book or a film… but a play?". I was amused by this and thought, "Haha! I'll show you!".

However, there was a more worrying feeling expressed that I could do nothing about – a sense of the interviews being too close to Dan's death. They had agreed, I think, to help Dan's parents' and their drama teacher's commitment to the project. I put my perception of their reservations to the back of my mind, and shepherded the interviews, with Izzy sitting silently (how did she manage that?) in the background throughout as 'safeguarding'. I found Izzy's presence supportive to me, given the wariness I sensed.

Jack (Dan's friend): My most palpable memory was the abject fear I felt as I walked out of my parents' car and into the church where Mark was waiting for his interviewees: it manifested very physically with a pulsing heat in my chest and a writhing of my stomach, which seemed to want to pull me away and back to the safety of my bedroom. But I knew on the other side of this struggle with my apprehension would be a gentle catharsis, an ability to tell my personal account of losing one of my favourite people. The fearful sensation did not fully subside during the interview; I was concerned both with telling Dan's story accurately, and maintaining a socially acceptable level of eye contact.

I remember thinking, and Jack's comment above is evidence of this, how unusually eloquent these young people were. The words in this play would be particularly potent.

Connie: Losing Dan was a tough season for all of us. I didn't particularly want to dwell on what happened too much. I had reservations at the time, that being interviewed would upset me again, but I focused on the bigger picture; to raise awareness about the dangers of drugs.

Another happy accident for me was Izzy's offer to some of the contributors to do their interviews in groups. What this inadvertently led to was snippets of natural conversations between them. It's something I now do as a preference. The difficulty was identifying different voices on my tape at home when transcribing, but now, with Zoom interviews, it is so much easier, as I can also see faces. This group chatter sometimes included me, so that was another decision I made early on… to include my own part in the interviews as I had done successfully in the later versions of *Race To Be Seen* and *Scratching The Surface*.

Bethany: I remember being super scared and nervous because I didn't want to say anything wrong, and it was all quite fresh. Mark made us feel so comfortable around such a delicate topic and it helped having Ms Forrester (legend) there to offer support. It was the first death many of us had experienced, so doing interviews about it was quite overwhelming, but I am grateful that I participated in the making of the play.

Jack: My motivation originally was a duty to Fiona, Tim, Jacob, Dan, and the story of his passing. As the only person both sober at the rave and willing to give an account of the events leading up to and following his death, I felt it was my duty to represent that very dark part of the story accurately during what was the darkest portion of my life so far. My reservations were about the intentions of the play: my overwhelming fear was that this personal tragedy would be used as an opportunity to make money, which so often happens. Time has proven this fear unfounded. The main purpose of the play (tirelessly executed) has been to spread the awareness of how important education is for teenagers, particularly on such fatal matters. I like to think my uncharacteristic diligence (as a lazy seventeen-year-old) in preserving the honesty of Dan's story has contributed to this spread.

Natasha (classmate of Dan): Before I came to Tenison's, I suffered with depression and mismanaged emotions. This led to substance abuse issues, among other things. When Dan passed I felt tremendous guilt, as there were times I could have faced the same fate, yet managed to narrowly escape. Dan had always been someone I had imagined older, still full of fun, still full of energy, and having achieved great success. When he passed it struck me that people are not invincible, and I realised my luck. I remember the interviews well. I worried that the stories we told, and our perception of Dan and what took place, whilst providing elucidation on the matter, may also rob the world and his family of the truth (a truth Dan alone could tell). I didn't want to taint his memory, nor the perception of his friends with him on the night. In particular, I didn't want people to believe that Dan must have been emotionally troubled or distressed for what happened to him to happen. It could have happened to anybody.

Megan: It was so important to his parents and to us. It kept Dan's memory alive and was a good excuse to keep talking about him. I was worried about maybe sharing things that his parents didn't know, but the story of his death is important for people to hear. You don't believe drugs will affect you or your friends until it does.

Izzy Forrester: The interviews were gruelling, to say the least. I will never forget that day. Hearing these young people, most of whom I had known for 5 years, so broken and confused, was awful. However, I was so proud of their words, their love for Dan, their funny memories and their compassion. As the day went on some became brave enough to say that Dan *had* taken MDMA previously. They were afraid of revealing this but were suffering terrible guilt that they had not said anything before. For me, this was particularly hard, as I realised I would have to tell Fiona and Tim (and soon) that their whole narrative around Dan's death would have to be experienced again and 're-written' in their minds and memories. I knew this would be devastating, especially as the young people most closely involved in the drug-taking had been constant visitors to the Spargo-Mabbs' home. I will never forget telling Fiona in her kitchen and the look in her eyes of confusion, and pain.

Fiona: The second time Mark came it was right after he'd spoken to Dan's friends. Izzy was with him, and she had to break it to Tim and me that there was a very different story, one we hadn't known anything about. I can't remember exactly what was said, but I can remember it felt like the incredibly fragile edifice that was life after Dan just shattered in pieces. I'd been working so hard to try to find, and hold tight to, the few random snatches of story I had, and piece them together to make some sort of sense of it all, and this threw them all up in the air and into the wind and I felt I was left with nothing. Who was this Dan? I'd lost my real Dan, and now I'd lost the Dan I thought I knew. I hadn't, of course, but Tim and I both felt like we had to begin grieving all over again, working out this different narrative, and finding Dan in it.

I was interviewing Jacob as Izzy was breaking the news to Fiona and Tim. I remember shifting in my chair so I wouldn't be distracted by whatever might occur in the kitchen. It was all incredibly 'real'.

Tim Spargo-Mabbs: I remember thinking at the time that the process of the writing of the play had itself become part of the process of the story coming out, and I was grateful, even though the new revelations made me feel as if the 'grieving clock' had been set back to the start. Then I waited as the interviews were painstakingly translated into a script over the coming months. I waited not knowing what to expect.

Chapter 4

FIRST DRAFT (1)

Some of Dan's friends expressed fears about younger people at their school presenting the premiere of this play which led to my gentle suggestion that OYT could take it on and would offer an emotional/geographical distance. We could also perform the official premiere at Tenison's. My suggestion pleased everyone and relieved some pressure for Izzy, and resolved my problem of OYTs next production! *I Love You, Mum – I Promise I Won't Die* (by this point that was the title) would be an eye-catching production. Directing it offered me an ongoing opportunity to hone it as had happened with so many of my most successful early plays.

My process in writing the play was to:
• transcribe the testimony
• put the transcripts into separate computer files
• edit the testimony to workable amounts (each hour of interview – 15k words – to be edited to under 5k words)
• select words to use in the play and highlight them in the edited testimony making it easy to check later if I had missed anything crucial

It really was that simple. I was strict about using only the words of those I had interviewed plus:
• an ambulance report.
• Fiona's victim statement for the sentencing of the dealer
• Fiona's background statement for the coroner
• an extract from Dan's memorial book written by his friends.

There was too much strong material for the one act play I had been commissioned to write so I offered a 'buy one, get one free' package ie to write two one act plays. I had developed a solid personal loyalty to the people and the project.

The revelation of the 'secret' (Dan having taken drugs previously) during the friends' interviews told me the friends and family stories intersected but also had totally separate elements. There would be information in the family's story the friends would not know, and vice-versa. I decided the play could be split exactly as my interviews were undertaken. Hope's interview took some thinking about, but I eventually decided to put her in the friends' story but to keep Fiona's contributions in as they had happened in the original interview.

This decided, I wanted to explore the most interesting way to tell this story (twice). In John Burgess' playwriting course, I mentioned earlier, I had been encouraged to explore 'structure'. This provided inspiration for *Chequered Flags to Chequered Futures*, which had two detailed accounts of one story played at different speeds, from two different perspectives. In performance, the play was impressive, and I preferred it to the more straightforward narrative storytelling of my early plays, such as *Too Much Punch For Judy*.

It is worth looking at *Chequered Flags* to examine the structure and how styles emerged to tell each side of the story. Chris' story (in every other scene) lent itself to an ensemble style, whereas Shelley's (the other scenes) were driven by powerful female monologues. A similar stylistic contrast worked for the two versions of Dan's story. The friends' story (*ILYM*) needed a larger, multi-rolling cast and demanded an imaginative, high-octane ensemble approach. The second half (*IPIWD*) required a more intimate, direct and naturalistic approach.

Having decided to include my questions in *ILYM* I consciously removed myself from *IPIWD* to allow the focus to remain exclusively on the people in the tragedy. Finally, I had to decide which play should be performed first. After much deliberation, I started with *ILYM* (predominantly so the energy of the performance grabs the audience's attention) and finished with a close-up on the family and girlfriends' family heart-wrenching recollections. The sacrifice I made by doing this was to exclude Fiona's shock when the friends make their revelation altering her understanding of her son's story.

I also wanted to introduce an interesting stylistic element to the play. Somehow my mind turned to recollections of a production of *Betrayal* by Harold Pinter. To be honest, I had not liked it but had adored the concept, where a marriage break-up is presented in reverse. I was convinced the idea of the narrative of the family story being told in reverse could work well. The audience already knew what had happened to Dan, so there was no sense of needing to keep that a secret. Telling the story backwards served to reflect the way in which I felt the family would go over and over the events, trying to trace them back to see what might have changed things… but at the same time hurtling towards the unchangeable tragic conclusion.

So, after the whole play was written (both parts running forward), I re-ordered the sections of what had become *IPIWD* and put them in reverse, deciding carefully where each break should be. This gave the play a circular structure which I remain proud of. There was another benefit to doing this: we could end with Fiona's final words to Daniel as he walked out that night (rather than his death) and then, in what is effectively an epilogue (these words were taken predominantly from Fiona's victim impact statement read out at the sentencing of the supplier), poignant images of Dan as an innocent child and baby, with the hopes and dreams lying ahead of him.

Fiona's final speech is one of the loveliest I have ever included in any of my plays.

This change happened as OYT progressed through rehearsals and was one of many where the cast had to suffer a radical alteration to what they had learnt. I wonder, would this have ever happened had we (OYT) not been premiering the play? I was nowhere near this point in November 2014 when I would have originally submitted the play for the planned February/March 2016 performances.

Chapter 5

EARLY (TESTIMONY) REHEARSALS

We had 30 plus people attend our first meeting, ranging in age from 11 to 20. None had heard of Dan, but all found information on the internet so were excited by the potential of the project.

Natascha Thomas (Fiona in the initial OYT production and the oldest (at 20), most experienced cast member): I had been involved in *Stop the Traffik*, and when I attended the first evening for that production I adored the idea of telling people's stories using their own words. After our success at the AETF (we won the English Final and went on to represent England in the British Final) I was hooked. When Mark introduced us to the story of Daniel, even without knowing Fiona and Tim, his family and friends, I wanted to help share this story. Knowing the freedom we had in OYT, I knew every person would be involved in generating a powerful, touching, sensitive, creative, and caring piece of theatre. I knew first-hand the effects drugs can have, so I would never have considered NOT being involved.

Emily Moulsdale (Kate in the original OYT production – Year 12 at the start): There was an overwhelming feeling of honour in being able to tell Dan's story through the words of his friends and family, even before having the final script.

Sally Britton (Hope in the original OYT production – Year 11 at the start and a rare non-Oasis student): The main attraction for me was that it hadn't been written. Being involved in mostly musical theatre companies from a young age, devising verbatim theatre offered a new and exciting concept to the 15 year-old me. It involved real lives, experiences and events of people of a very similar age to myself, so I felt as if I could help keep the truth, as I could relate to, and see myself in, very similar situations to Dan and his friends.

Chelsea Fisher (Bridget in the original OYT production – Year 11 at the start): I hadn't been in an OYT production previously but did know their reputation. Mark, who was my Drama teacher, let us know what his upcoming play was about. Having family members affected by similar things, I felt that going along to get more information was a must.

I remember knowing this was something that could save and change lives. Had it been created just a few years before, it may have saved a life in my family. If it could do the same for others, I wanted to be a part of it!

Many of those who came forward to be in the cast for the production had little experience. This was not a concern to me (it never was), and possibly dates back to something that happened in my own final schooldays.

As the Head Boy of our House, I had taken it upon myself to run a production group putting on self-written musicals in my final year at school. They had proved popular and successful. At the end of that year my Head of House (teacher) asked if I would 'manage' the 1st year (Year 7) sports team on Sports Day. I was excited by the prospect, as I knew some of them from the productions, and they seemed excited to have me as their manager. I had no idea what their sporting abilities were.

The day arrived, and using all my skills to motivate and enthuse, we all had a great day together, and ended up winning by quite a margin. I will never know whether this was a quirk of their extreme ability or my 'management skills'. I decided it was the latter, and cite this as a watershed moment for me; it didn't matter who I worked with, but if we all worked together, in harmony, and with a common goal – nothing can stop us. Consequently, having a Youth Theatre where many have no real experience does not phase me. I also had the benefit of a few older ones with experience who were able to become effectively additional assistant directors, leading by example. Everyone was committed to 'believe'. I explored another important element contributing to this lack of concern about experience in my recent book about developing verbatim plays and is worth revisiting here:

'The focus in my productions was always on the story we were telling, rather than on how good we were (or weren't). It shifted the perspective of both cast members and audience. People have said to me how professional my youth theatre casts were and I was often asked how we did it. I never had a definitive answer, but I now realise it was our focus on these real people and their stories, rather than on ourselves, that enabled us to lose the self-consciousness that tends to befall (poor) student theatre.' *Verbatim – The Fun of Making Theatre Seriously* by Mark Wheeller (2021), Salamander Street

Amy Sturrock (Megan in the original OYT production – Year 11 at the start, a non-Oasis student but with a family who were deeply engrained in OYT): I felt an overwhelming pressure to make sure I and everyone else was doing justice to Dan's story. Their 'presence' (regardless of whether they were there in reality or not) made me work harder and be more dedicated. I had worked with OYT on projects before this, and I can say confidently that it's the one I'm most proud of, as we saw the reactions to this story they generously allowed us to tell.

Ollie Webb (Ensemble in the original OYT production, boy on the cover of the script and youngest cast member – Year 7 at the start): Mark spoke to me one lunch time, and said he'd love me to be involved. I had watched a few OYT plays and at primary school had worked with Mark in Junior OYT so had a good understanding of what it was about, as well as a strong interest in Drama. I knew whatever I was getting myself into would be great. The first few sessions were scary – new people, older people (SOOO much older), and, as I saw it, a lot of talented people. As a young person of eleven, drugs, grief, bereavement etc, were things I hadn't come across previously. I often remember a real sense of emotion in the room.

For the first few meetings the cast worked with the unedited testimony (which is all I had) to become familiar with the material before I had a completed script. This was valuable in three main respects:

1/ it separated the wheat from the chaff – those who would have the resilience and commitment to work on something with such a long lead time and no immediate performance gratification

2/ it offered an opportunity to generate clear, stylistic ways of working with the testimony, which we could apply throughout the next year of rehearsals

3/ everyone developed a robust working relationship with each other.

Chelsea Fisher (Bridget in the original OYT production – Year 11 at the start): We were passed pages upon pages of unedited testimony written out word for word from the recorded interviews. I remember thinking 'I don't know how I am going to do this without crying'. This wasn't just a play. I was aware of that as soon as we started to read the testimony.

Central to my approach was a determination to find theatricality for every scene. It is verbatim theatre… not just verbatim! I have seen so many lazy professional (never amateur, strangely) verbatim theatre productions where the 'theatre' bit is forgotten, with people sitting/standing and delivering lines with no discernible movement. Imaginative presentation was a central tenet to everything I had been involved in, and continued to be throughout our preparation for this production (and beyond!).

Lewis Evans: (Jack in the original OYT production – Year 11 at the start): It enabled us to experience the words. It was an incredibly different experience to how I had previously worked. We spent a fair amount of time as an ensemble exploring exactly the type of theatre that we wanted to produce.

Alysha-Jade Patis (Connie in the original OYT production – Year 10 at the start): I remember having loads of pieces of paper with different testimonies and trying to make these into theatre. I hadn't had much drama experience, but what I did know was not what we were doing. I knew Drama as getting a script, learning the lines, and performing it the way the stage directions told you to. This was another thing altogether! There were absolutely no stage directions. There were so many fillers ('um's and 'er's) and, although completely natural in speech, being told when to say them felt odd.

Sally Britton (Hope in the original OYT production – Year 11 at the start): We were put into groups and got stuck into creating snapshots of the testimonies, rather like a montage of past memories. Each week the testimonies were cut or reordered, which was annoying as our ideas would have to be changed or scrapped, but this was actually a useful process ie not getting stuck on one idea. We didn't hear the interview recordings for several weeks. I remember hearing the words I had read on the recording and the resonance was so much deeper and heartfelt. It gave me a determination to give these words truth and meaning. Not only were they more emotional, but sometimes more comical, which gave so much more of a lightness to our work.

From early on, I had offered Natascha and James (the two oldest – 19/20 year olds – and most experienced members of OYT) the roles of Fiona and Tim. On December 15th they both met Tim and Fiona, who had agreed to drop in on the way home from a short break they'd had in Swanage. I took the opportunity on this visit to show Tim and Fiona extracts from the OYT DVD of *Too Much Punch For Judy* (25th anniversary production), which not only showed them how these plays are staged imaginatively but also what an amazing performer Natascha is… she had played Jo in that production! Natascha sent me this message that evening.

Natascha Thomas (Fiona in the original OYT production – in a message to Mark Wheeller 15th Dec 2014): Meeting Tim and Fiona, a strong-willed couple with a gaping hole in their life, gave me confidence to do this heartfelt piece for them. I know this will give great support to the family and friends of Dan, and we will have just as much in return from them. It has opened my eyes to how real this is. This isn't just a play we're putting on, it is someone's life, and we need to respect that in every way possible. We have a great reputation, let's keep that up, and prove they have chosen to do the right thing by using us to keep Dan and his story alive, and make young people aware of the dangers of drug misuse. Thank you, Mark, so much, for the opportunity of meeting this wonderful couple. I'm honoured to help share their story.

The best way of motivating my Youth Theatre groups was always to set up a situation where they can produce work beyond what they believe they are capable of. Verbatim theatre projects achieve this because they tell highly motivating stories. I started with telling Graham Salmon's (the world's fastest blind athlete) at Epping Youth Theatre in 1984. Fiona and Tim seemed to embrace our group just as Graham had at EYT and, of course, Natascha (and James) talked to the other cast members, raising their aspirations for what we might achieve.

Lewis Evans (Jack in the original OYT production – Year 11 at the start): I remember first meeting Fiona and Tim. We were invited to their house, a surreal experience, bearing in mind I was only 16, not far off the age of Dan when the awful event happened. I remember thinking this could have been me, my best friend or anyone. We were there to get family videos of when Dan was very young. Little did we know, but Hope and Jack were also invited to meet us, and that was terrifying. I felt very out of place asking them questions about what had happened. I look back and think how incredible, mature and mind-blowingly strong they were amidst the anger, sadness and other emotions they endured. Breath-taking.

Chapter 6

FIRST DRAFT (2)

I had never had a positive experience of a read-through as a Youth Theatre director until this play. For our previous production, *Silas Marner*, I decided not to have one, for fear it might put people off being involved. Instead, I introduced the play scene by scene, week by week as we came to rehearse it. This idea worked wonderfully, setting up excitement for the start of each rehearsal for the cast to see what happened next in the story. My experience of first read-throughs was cast members stumbling through words and everything seeming so slow that I would return home depressed and feeling I had to edit and re-write extensively. On 3rd March 2015, when I had completed the play, I ploughed on with a table read. I wanted to risk it so everyone could see how I had organised the testimony they were already becoming familiar with.

Amy Sturrock (Megan in the original OYT production – Year 11 at the start): I remember the first read-through vividly. It was incredibly powerful, with tears, laughter and so much emotion throughout the room. It was one of the most moving experiences I've ever been part of. It was hard to process, knowing these were people's real thoughts/feelings. More than ever, I wanted to ensure they were portrayed truthfully.

Lewis Evans (Jack in the original OYT production – Year 11 at the start): The first read-through gave everyone new-found drive and an even greater reason to tell this story. The powerful words (that had only been heard in small, non-linear extracts), were pieced together so we could understand the weight of such an incredibly important message.

Alysha-Jade Patis (Connie in the original OYT production – Year 10 at the start): Wow! Seeing the testimonies put into a script with a timeline and a concept was so, so powerful. The words were so heartfelt and warming there was not a dry eye. I don't cry reading words on a page, but this was so much more than that. By the end I felt like I knew Dan.

Carley Sefton-Wilson (Assistant Director, OYT): The graphic details regarding Dan's death worried me. How could we show it sensitively while still showing the magnitude of what he and his family suffered? I also worried about the cast. Some were quite young, and I remember watching their faces as Dan's dying was described. I think when you hear of drug deaths in the press, it's normally a headline, 'Young Person Dies Taking Drugs', but when we read what Dan's body went through in the hours before he died, some of the cast looked visibly shaken. I was also worried about the other young contributors to the play, and the relationship with his different friendship groups. I was aware it all had to be handled with such sensitivity. The last thing we would want was to cause more suffering to people who had been through so much. In the end, I think we did this very well.

Sally Britton (Hope in the original OYT production – Year 11 at the start): I remember the first reading very clearly. We read through and it brought a large number of us to tears. The words were so powerful. We had an audition process... I cannot remember how that happened?

The 'audition process' was interesting and conducted in a way I'd never used so fully in previous productions. We'd been working together for four months. People had been playing someone different each week, apart from Natascha and James (Fiona and Tim). I feared making final decisions would separate the group into those who had the major parts and those who didn't, and in turn, that may cause a cast fall-out. I didn't know what to do, but as everything thus far had been so democratic, I decided to open out the experience; everyone could do an 'audition' and everyone could have a say in who was the best fit for that part, including pushing for themselves to play such and such a role for whatever reason. And that's what happened. It worked surprisingly well, and decisions were made with no great disagreements as I remember. It was an unusually smooth way of conducting the whole thing. A nice surprise! Bizarrely, none of the cast who sent their memories remembered the auditions, so they clearly didn't make much of an impression! And there was me thinking... how radical!

Sally Britton (Hope in the original OYT production – Year 11 at the start): After getting our parts I focused more on Hope. I was able to follow her on Instagram/add her on Facebook despite never having met her before. This was the weirdest concept to me. I was nervous she would think I was a stalker or was invading her privacy, but she was the loveliest person, and very accepting and open to sharing ideas and being involved in the piece, because it was the first time we were performing it. We became almost like online pen-pals, and it gave me a really good insight into her as a person as opposed to a fictional character.

Hope: I've been contacted by several students playing my 'character' (since Hope) in the play, which has been insensitive. It's important to understand how young we were when it happened, but that also comes with a lack of understanding from those who are taking part in the play now. If they really understood what it was like to lose a friend at 16, they wouldn't contact me and ask for advice on how to 'play the character'. It's not just a play, it's our lives.

Hope's contact with Sally was negotiated via Fiona and myself and was part of our process. However Hope references the terminology I have used at the front of the script ie being a 'character'. I totally agree with Hopes reservations about that term. Regrettably, I listed the contributors as 'characters' at the start of the published play. I did this purely because that is what always happens in published plays. That said, I remember the first time I handed one of my plays (*Too Much Punch For Judy*) to a professional director and, an early discussion we had concerning the idea of Judy being a 'character', as they were preparing for their performance:

'He ripped into Judy's 'guilt complex' and how this affects the playing of her 'character'. He kept referring to her as a 'character'. Toni (Judy) being a real person seemed to be an inconvenience to him. It was blocking his 'artistic' endeavours. I fear they plan to portray Toni more unsympathetically than we did. He refuses to meet her, arguing that it would detrimentally affect their opportunities to 'interpret her character'.'
From *The Story Behind Too Much Punch For Judy* by Mark Wheeller

I did have an understanding that this was the wrong terminology yet, oddly, continued to use it in the published play text. Interestingly, I note in the verbatim plays I self-published ('Scratching the Surface' and 'Can You Hear Me Major Tom?') I have not done this, referring to them as 'Cast'. I will remember this for the future, and ensure the term 'characters' is not used. I agree with Hope; they are real people. That said, Jack, another contributor, made this comment, and referred to himself as a 'character' in the play. Interesting, eh?

Jack: Frankly, I have made efforts to distance myself from the play, as I do not possess the necessary faculties to compartmentalise my emotions. While I am happy that the play will grow and touch many hearts and ignite many conversations, I am also happy to keep my distance and let the fragment of me that belongs there to remain in the character of 'Jack'. I want something good to come from this very, very bad thing.

Chapter 7

MEETING

In April, Fiona and Tim met the cast and watched the opening scene, which included the rave in which Daniel dies. This threw everyone in at the deep end but was something that needed to happen at some stage. (I remember doing this successfully with Graham Salmon asking EYT to show him, on their first meeting with him, the scene where his parents were informed that their baby's eyes were to be removed due to his otherwise incurable cancer.) I saw no merit in delaying it and looked forward to the intensity of the meetings. However, I was only too aware it would be very different from the perspective of Dan's family. I had complete confidence in my young (and in some cases inexperienced) cast and the positive impression they would make. Young people are the best!

Fiona: I remember that first meeting at Oasis Academy Lords Hill. I wanted to bring Dan to them somehow, so they'd feel they knew him, and would get him as right as they could. I wasn't sure how to do this, though. Then I had the idea of taking a bag of his shoes – the scruffy old school shoes he somehow always managed to wear out in just the same places, the new ones he'd only had chance to wear for ten days, the Converse he inherited from Jacob, the 'old man's slippers' (as he called them) that he loved to slouch around in at home with his comfy dressing gown, and so on. All of them said something about Dan, had a story that said something about who he was. The young people in the cast were all so, so lovely. From that first meeting we could see they were so committed to what they were doing, so concerned to do it all as well as they could, to get it all as right as they could, and seemed genuinely to care about Dan, and about us, and we quickly came to care so much about them, and feel very connected to them all through this process of recreating the story of our son.

Chelsea Fisher (Bridget in the original OYT production – Year 11 at the start): I remember the first time Tim and Fiona came to our rehearsal. Everybody sat in a circle and completely focused on their every word. They brought his shoes with them so we could see a small part of Dan. I still cry today when I think of this. Dan's passing was so recent yet they managed to work through such horrific pain and put others first. Their story hurt them to share but they were aware it could save others. We could see the pain that watching rehearsals or speaking to us caused them. They became a huge inspiration and to this day I think of them often!

Tim: Meeting the OYT cast for the first time remains etched in my memory as one of the half dozen most intense experiences of my life. It felt as if community was growing between us like the tendrils of a vine as we watched, and they acted, and then we all got together in a circle to share how we were all finding it. It was a defining moment for me. I was very touched that these lovely, earnest young people were so keen to do right by us. That earnestness was its own reward as far as I'm concerned. My brother, Russ, had asked to drive us down and I had no idea why he would want to. As so often, I had factored in the practical elements of the visit but not the emotional elements. I didn't know what to expect at all. Afterwards, being driven home, I totally got why Russ had wanted to drive us. I was high as a kite and flat as a pancake. He, Fiona and I talked long and hard about the emotional depths/heights, and the mystical way this seemed to bring us all together.

Chelsea Fisher (Bridget in the original OYT production – Year 12): Having Fiona and Tim there while we performed actually made it harder for me. It wasn't that we put in more or less effort but I almost felt slightly guilty that what we were doing was causing them to have to relive the hardest time of their lives. For this reason, I always wanted to make sure they were not going through such pain all over again for nothing. They did not need to be in the room for me to feel this way. Every time I stood on stage, entrusted with Dan's memories, I wanted to ensure I was doing all I could to tell his story as well as he deserved it to be told.

Ollie Webb (Ensemble in the original OYT production, boy on the cover of the script – Year 7 at the start): Meeting Tim and Fiona was an emotional experience. It felt like we knew these people very well already. They instantly became all of our mum and dads, and were so lovely to share their story with us. A strong memory is the first time we showed them the rave scene. I remember the part where I (as Dan) get thrown forward and drop to the floor. I crawl slowly towards a block, down stage right. I remember looking up and making eye contact with Fiona, and she began to sob. That was the lowest point for me in the whole process of *ILYMIPIWD*. Playing Dan at what was his most vulnerable point was very difficult. It was a point that Tim and Fiona would have never seen in reality, and knowing I was the one to portray him was a big weight on my shoulders – something that emotionally I struggled with a lot. Deep grief and bereavement were feelings I had not had to deal with yet at that young age, however, I was having to perform something very poignant. It was very, very difficult for me at times, but I wouldn't change my experience for anything. If anything, I should thank you (Mark) for putting me in a little bit of a vulnerable situation.

Fiona: They'd prepared just the opening rave scene at that stage, and watching this was agonising. The cast was amazing, but what they were portraying – the rave, the excitement, it all going horribly wrong for Dan – was something I'd imagined so many times, but not really seen even in my head, and not like that. To see Dan in his last conscious moments embodied on stage, crawling along on his stomach, looking in so much pain, and so scared and lost, was awful. Awful, awful, awful. I just wanted to get out of the room, but I knew the young cast members were so conscious of Dan's mum and dad watching, and I really didn't want to distract them, or disappoint them, or disrupt their performance, but at some point the sob I'd been holding in reached such a pitch I had to rush out (as undramatically as I could). There were several visits over the following months as they worked on their production, and we saw various scenes as they developed.

Carley Sefton-Wilson (Assistant Director, OYT): I remember how quickly Fiona and Tim fitted into the group. The cast were so respectful and I felt so proud that such a young cast handled a situation which could have been difficult so well. Tim and Fiona brought such honesty when they were in the room that we were all in awe of them. I remember being almost overwhelmed when Tim spoke at times. The way he has with words made us all listen. What made our version of the play so special was the relationship Tim and Fiona created with James and Tasha. It must be very strange to watch somebody portray you on stage. It must be even more difficult to see them act out the most awful aspects of your life, but the support they showed James and Tasha helped them to develop their portrayal so much. I remember speaking to Tasha regarding what it was like to have Fiona in the room, and she said at first she was really nervous, but actually Fiona was so lovely to her that she just wanted to make her character more lovely to show what Fiona was like in real life. In the end Tim, Fiona and Jacob became part of OYT. We loved having them there. It never felt difficult. We were aware of the pain and grief they were suffering, which made us all the more determined to do it justice and produce a play which not only honoured Dan's memory, but showed their journey honestly so the world could see how amazing they are. I remember being really moved when I saw on the anniversary of Dan's death a lot of the cast lit candles and posted them on their social media in memory of Dan. This wasn't just about an OYT production but about a group of young people becoming part of a drug education campaign.

Chapter 8

REHEARSAL PROCESS

I am aware students have to understand what our rehearsal process was so asked the cast contributors to this book about this but firstly, I will include what I believe to be the best description of how I work with my casts, written by a couple of OYT members for my *Verbatim – The Fun of Making Theatre Seriously* book.

Simon Froud (An OYT member for many years prior to this production): Throughout the years of working with Mark, I've realised he only knows one way of directing, which is simply not to direct. Instead, he acts as a curator to the ideas in the room, shaping, evolving, destroying, rejecting and embellishing them. As a director (and as an educator), Mark is more of a guide. He is a curator not a director.

Charlotte McGuinness Shaw (A former OYT member from 'Silas Marner'): 'This could work. Let's try it' is the best way to explain the process of *Silas Marner*. Every suggestion is discussed and tried, whether it be from a chorus member or the protagonist. Quite often the original idea doesn't work, but another suggestion will stem from that, and the process continues with the entire cast having the chance of an input. What is suggested by one person won't be the complete answer, but it starts the process off, and as more and more cast members add suggestions, with Mark's guidance, the idea is transformed into this amazingly clever piece of theatre. As the rehearsals go on, there are more and more amazingly clever moments of theatre created, until suddenly, at the dress rehearsal, we realise we have tweaked and pasted everything together into one amazingly clever play.

Here are the *ILYMIPIWD* contributors' responses regarding their perception of our rehearsal process. I hope it helps to understand our way of working:

Conner Handstock (An Assistant Director in the final months of the rehearsals): Mark didn't set things in stone until late in the rehearsal process. He liked the concept of 'play' and 'exploration'. Often he would give the young actors a task, or a prop, or something he'd like them to achieve, and off they went, searching for answers, creating new possibilities, building foundations, tearing them down and reshaping them until settling on something. That 'something' would then be refined, with or without Mark's direction, until that scene or moment in the play was operating like clockwork. Even then, Mark wouldn't be afraid to change or adapt if there was a call for that to happen. With regards to staging, it was always purposeful and minimalistic.

Alysha-Jade Patis (Connie in the original OYT production – Year 11): The process was very, very long. We worked collaboratively. We had a 'director' but we were all directors, free to interpret and try different ideas. We would often split into smaller groups with a scene each (sometimes groups working on the same scene) and then stage it and bring it to life. We would watch each other's scenes and discuss what we liked/didn't like and make creative decisions from there.

Chelsea Fisher (Bridget in the original OYT production – Year 12): Some nights we would spend hours going over one small scene again and again. If something wasn't right, we would work together to find something that did work. If you weren't in the scene being looked at that night, you pulled up a chair and watched, so there were more perceptions to help resolve the issue. We were able to give our opinions and thoughts and have them heard, and that created a feeling of being more than just someone performing the play. I felt truly involved and had the deepest attachment to it.

Lewis Evans: (Jack in the original OYT production – Year 12): The exploration and rehearsal process were unlike anything I'd experienced before. We were asked to think, 'Was there a new mood to the scene? And if so, what caused it?' We would build from there. It was devised from improvisation and exploration. The creative process was organic, fresh and 'in the moment'. There was no 'planning'.

Emily Moulsdale (Kate in the original OYT production – Year 13): Even when we had something good, we remained determined to turn it into something amazing and use different styles of acting. Our open approach to change was imperative. I remember Mark left us with the script and let us decide how to stage certain scenes before coming back to see what we had come up with, and only then adding his expertise to our creation.

Ollie Webb (Ensemble in the original OYT production, boy on the cover of the script – Year 8): OYT didn't work how I expected. It was a not "Director and Cast" as two separate units. We worked together to create something outstanding. The scene that stood out most for me was the scene where I played Dan at the rave, and was thrown around by the rest of the cast. This developed from a piece of music which created an atmosphere and we worked from there. I come from a dance background, so this allowed me to indulge being launched across the stage. The scene took time to create the perfect version of what a stylised rave might look like. We wanted to imitate how Dan would feel in that moment. It needed to be a sensory overload. The movement had to be high-paced and travel around the space resulting in a sudden contrasting halt! The scene was created through trust between me as the person being lifted and thrown, and the rest of the cast who were throwing, lifting and catching me… most of the time haha!

One thing Ollie didn't mention is that I would bring 'experts' in to assist us where possible. For the scene he described above, I brought in an ex-OYT member (Matt Savage), an experienced hip-hop dancer who had experience I did not have of raves. He came to a session and helped develop the scene in a manner I could never have mustered. We also had a whole day workshop with Tim Ford, currently the Artistic Director of the Gatehouse Theatre in Stafford, and an 'expert' working on my plays.

Alysha-Jade Patis (Connie in the original OYT production – Year 11): We had workshops with professional practitioners who brought life to what we had created and gave us more amazing ideas to work with. Tim Ford wanted us to include water bottles and led to one of the most vital parts of the show. He dotted the stage with numerous water bottles and had us move around them while doing our scenes. This didn't actually end up happening, but it inspired something else. It was the idea of trying anything and everything that stuck with me.

Chelsea Fisher (Bridget in the original OYT production – Year 12): Working with Tim Ford was a great experience. We had been rehearsing the play for a while at this point when we already felt very attached to the plays ('ILYM' & 'IPIWD') themselves but also the people involved. Tim brought in a fresh pair of eyes. He took amazing scenes and added a fresh dynamic. He was able to detach slightly and focus on small details that helped us bring scenes together more visually.

Sally Britton (Hope in the original OYT production – Year 12): Ollie came up with the idea of holding his phone light under the bottle that made it glow in the dark and stand out. This looked amazing and so that stuck. I use vitamin C drinks a lot, and had the idea of using them as the tablet. When they dissolve, they fizz and glow in a colour. Phones were difficult to hold under the bottle, and the timing of turning on your torch on was sloppy, so we introduced little LED handheld lights.

Carley Sefton Wilson (Assistant Director OYT): There were key moments where we could see it coming together. The night we developed the idea of the bottle lighting felt like a huge breakthrough. We did

this by showing Dan and his friends standing in a line after they bought the drugs, each holding a bottle of water. They mimed tipping the drugs into the water and pressing a small thumb-light under each one to light it up. When Dan put his drugs in the bottle, it lit up red. This was a brilliant moment to show whoever had taken that pill would have died, just like in roulette. It took a while to develop the idea. The cast embraced this approach and I'm so proud of how they put Dan's memory at the centre of what they did. None had ever met Dan, yet at times it felt like he was a friend when they talked about how to portray him on stage.

George Davis (Harvey in the original OYT production – Year 10 at the start): Sometimes Mark would direct us if he had a clear vision of what he wanted, but he would also step back so we could come up with something to present to him. Whichever way, both the cast and Mark would use this to bounce ideas off each other. It worked well. The rehearsal periods could be stressful. We would rework scenes to make them better or fine tune them. When the set came in, it started coming together. The boxes were great. We were able to move the set around how we wanted so much more easily.

Chapter 9

SET DESIGN

Richard Long (Set designer for the original OYT production):
I was invited by Mark to work on his new play following my previous involvement in two of his other plays, *Jack* and *Silas Marner*. After the briefing, I realised this was to be like no other play I had worked on. After an emotional meeting with Dan's family I knew that any input I had would need to be sensitive and respectful, as this tragic event was still very much in the present. I took inspiration from a performance I had seen a few years previously of Maresa von Stockert's *Grimm Desires*, a contemporary dance performance based on Grimm's *Fairy Tales*. I was fascinated by the limited use of set.

The performers had their costume, a few props, and were carefully illuminated in a dark setting so that the audience's entire focus was on the performer. Mark had suggested a minimal set design to allow the performers to be the main focus. We had discussed simple blocks and screens, painted white, that were not too big and easy to move on stage and also easily transportable. I suggested the use of pull up banners, the type used in schools for open evenings, but blank/plain white or maybe with selected words from the script printed on them. We also discussed the use of coloured or flashing lights projected onto the set, for example during the rave scene.

By chance, while these ideas were going through my head, I saw an advert online for garden furniture showing a group of young people sitting on a garden patio on white plastic cubes. The cubes had a light inside that could change colour to suit the mood and also a strobe effect. All of this could all be controlled by a remote control. Immediately I thought, 'These could be used in the play!' A different colour to suit each scene, the strobe effect for the rave scene, and they were compact and easy to transport. No chairs nor any other set needed. The illuminated cubes could be used to set the scene and as uplighters in a darkened space. Mark liked the idea and early trials proved successful, once we had settled on a plan for controlling all the lights at the right moment.

Amy Sturrock (Megan in the original OYT production – Year 12): I remember the cubes arriving and the excitement of what we could create with them. They became imperative to the play.

Alysha-Jade Patis (Connie in the original OYT production – Year 11): We had 6 light up cubes which we tried to incorporate into every scene. Sometimes this was easy, they became chairs, but after a while that becomes boring. So, in the rave scene they became symbolic of the drugs. We slammed our hands on them and breathed in audibly, and then stood up and exhaled even more loudly. This was a way of showing us taking drugs, and setting the scene at a festival, without actually standing there and swallowing a pill or sniffing something up your nose. Another scene where we questioned what to do with the blocks was the funeral scene. The cast on stage were stood as you are at a funeral, so the blocks were on stage with no purpose, then we came up with the idea of carrying the blocks as though they were the coffin, and placing them down 'into the ground'. This kind of idea helped to add layers to the scene.

Chelsea Fisher (Bridget in the original OYT production – Year 12): I wondered how the production could be improved with costumes and set. It felt like we could stand in a line and read the script and it would still have such an emotional impact on the audience. The words carried the play. I was concerned that anything added on that might feel overwhelming. The colour changing cubes were so subtly used that they highlighted the emotions of the play and us on stage. They were a perfect enhancement to the words.

Chapter 10

MULTIMEDIA DESIGN

Danny Sturrock (Lighting and Multimedia Design): I had recently completed a degree in Television & Video Post-Production and around this time had developed an interest in using projection mapping in a theatrical setting – and this was one of the first suggestions I made to Mark. He did not have the faintest idea what I was talking about, but once I explained it he seemed excited by the suggestions I made as to how it could be incorporated.

Initially I envisaged having a minimalistic set comprising stackable/ easy to move blocks to create various shapes and platforms onto which video could then be projected, creating an ever-changing digital set. I set to work testing out various programs we could use for the projection mapping, and a few weeks later myself and Mark met with Richard Long to brainstorm more set design ideas.

Richard had created a scale model for us to play around with so we could start to envisage how the blocks would work in reality. During this meeting it dawned on me that, as there was now mention of the play being performed in other locations outside our Academy, with the potential for the premiere to be held in Croydon, having a complex digital set could be problematic.

Another idea could be just having a large, static projection screen, but to me this wasn't an innovative approach, and in OYT we always strived to try new things and push our creative boundaries. I eventually settled on having the option of being able to utilise projection mapping onto six small pop-up screens or a single large static screen, so we would have options to cater for different performance spaces. The video content I produced was designed to highlight locations or key events within the plays, from something as simple as a static image projected of a magistrates' court crest set against a grey wall, to more complex compositions depicting the rave at the warehouse, which changed and altered as the tension in those scenes built to their conclusion.

The lighting design was influenced by the inclusion of light cubes that made up the staging, and a clever use of light via water bottles, effervescent vitamin C tablets and thumb-button torches. These elements of light which the cast had created during the workshop period were visually stunning and therefore any additional lighting would only need to light the actors on stage sufficiently to be seen, without being concerned with creating mood and atmosphere, as this was being achieved through the actors, the staging, video content and of course the music.

The lighting design was therefore simple and consisted of various areas of general cover with little use of colour, except for the rave and the funeral scene, which were both backlit with a blue wash to compliment the video content, mood and lights used by the cast. The approach of less is more in terms of lighting was right for this project as no one element overpowered another, and I feel part of the success of this piece was the seamless integration of all visual and audio design elements. It is one of the productions I am most proud of in terms of the visual design elements.

Emily Moulsdale (Kate in the original OYT production – Year 13): I remember the light up boxes arriving and being excited as I could picture how effective they would be, especially in the rave scene, but the most powerful moment was having the videos of Dan as a child. I remember vividly the emotion felt by all when we first saw these.

Natasha Thomas (Fiona in the original production): When we first worked with the multimedia we felt our hard work finally coming together and the atmosphere changed. The videos on the multimedia made every scene more difficult, as we needed to ensure we were in time and tightened our work rather than added to it, but this is when our 'performance' was truly birthed.

Chapter 11

MUSICAL UNDERSCORE

Built into the multimedia was what I consider to be the most creative story of all the backstage contributions... the musical underscore by Paul Ibbott. Paul had written the wonderful music for *Too Much Punch For Judy* (25th anniversary production). Somehow the story behind the music on this production has remained untold until now... so, as an exclusive for this book, I am delighted that Paul has offered to reveal the full story:

> **Paul Ibbott (Composer/Musical Director for the original OYT production):** A piece of music is like a life. It begins as nothing more than an idea in the silence. It develops and grows, and it impacts the environment. It gives some people immense pleasure. It annoys others. And yet other people may find it has a spiritual significance that may or may not be widely understood. And, just like a life, the music ends in silence. My first encounter with Fiona Spargo-Mabbs took place at a meeting of OYT, convened to hear her tell her story of Dan. She told of who he was and what he was like, and the way she told it was like a piece of music. Its impact and spiritual significance to me were immense. I remember crying as I related it to my wife later – not because it was sad, but because it was brimful of love. I started composing the music from silence. The story of Dan was in my head but no music. So, I began looking for techniques to help generate ideas. I remembered classical composers, such as Bach, created motifs using musical cryptograms, whereby musical notes represent letters of the alphabet.

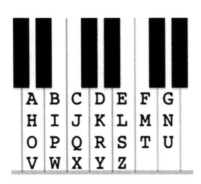

I played the notes for Dan (D-A-G) and immediately found a motif I liked. I used the same process for Dan S-M (D-A-G-E-F), Fiona (F-Bb-A-G-A), Jacob (C-A-C-A-Bb) and Tim (F-Bb-F) and found I could weave them together in different ways, which I thought was an interesting metaphor for the relationships in a family.

In addition, I was given a piece of dance music (Tiki Coronation) composed by Dan's friend, Jack Scott. It is evocative and exciting and deserved to play a central role in the musical story, and I was excited to find that it was in the same key as the ideas I had been developing. This meant I could easily create ideas that would move seamlessly in and out of Jack's piece. I worked out motifs for Jack (C-A-C-D) and for others of his friends, determined to use as many of them as I could.

However, I still had no idea how these motifs would fit with the play, as it was still being devised. There was a script (subject to many, many changes!) but the energy of the play would come from the cast through the rehearsal process. To make musical progress with this, I attended cast rehearsals and filmed sections of the play in early stages of development. Then I imported the film into Logic Pro, which allowed me to synchronise musical ideas and changes to key parts of the script and action, as I saw them. As the script and performances were refined and polished, so too the timings and dynamics of the music became more precise. When characters were on stage together, I would often combine or juxtapose their motifs, and nearly always layer them with one or other of Dan's motifs, since they were invariably recalling events in Dan's life.

I was consciously emphasising the energy levels and mood of the performance rather than leading it, but there were a couple of occasions where I felt the music needed to deliberately lead a change in intensity. The first was the build-up to the rave where the dynamics of the music rise, causing the cast to raise their voices, climaxing with the loud, energetic, almost frantic Tiki Coronation. The second occasion occurs twice: the music stops completely. It may be strange to hear, but I was particularly pleased when a festival adjudicator, giving the music and lighting a technical award, highlighted that the effect of the music stopping was especially striking because it intensified the feelings of tragedy, loss and shock.

The relationship between an underscore and a play/film is interesting. For much of a play, if you notice it, the music may well have failed in its job. On the other hand, its presence as one of the layers of story-telling ought to enrich the experience of the audience. If it doesn't, it is certainly better that there is no music.

As an addendum to this I would like to add that during our preparation period my musical hero, David Bowie, died. As a little tribute to him I included his *Everyone Says Hi* song as the final pre-show song and sign to the cast that the play was about to open. The lyrics were intended as a tribute to his own father (or Marc Bolan – or both) but I felt they could equally be applied to Dan. When I approached Fiona with the idea she liked it (and the song).

Chapter 12

HOODIE

One of the key dates in our timetable was a performance to Dan's family and friends in December 2015. We had prepared the play to a point where we could present it but our plans were shattered the week before. Harry, who played Dan, was becoming a successful kickboxer with international possibilities opening up for him. Fight dates were arising that conflicted with our rehearsal requirements and, understandably, challenged Harry's ability to commit to the production. He was prevaricating but I needed certainty and pushed him towards a decision, which I sensed was about to be made anyway. He didn't want to leave us in the lurch but I said,

"We need to resolve this problem sooner rather than later, and cancelling this private performance is a pain… but it won't be the end of the world".

Over a year into our project, we were suddenly without our central actor. The obvious solution was to find a replacement, but who should it be? Do we cast from within, meaning we have to also replace the replacement, or do we draft someone in from outside and give them the 'star role'? Also, how would Fiona and Tim respond to us finding someone else and have to build a relationship with them, as they had with Harry?

Danny had been packing up the tech equipment as I was having my conversation with Harry. Danny knew what was happening and he looked up at me and said something along the lines of: "You know that out of this you will think of something amazing… and that will be the best thing for the production." I went home knowing I had to be imaginative… and I was! Necessity is the mother of invention.

> **Lewis Evans (Jack in the original OYT production – Year 12):**
> When Harry left, I felt disheartened and confused as to how someone could want to leave the project in its final stages and remember thinking, "Will anybody else want to leave?".

My response was crucial. I couldn't risk it becoming a tsunami of departure. I needed to react fast. I was aware that some cast members had little to do and this situation offered an opportunity for more involvement, something everyone would appreciate. I wanted to find a way to share Dan's role amongst them but I needed a device to let the audience know who was playing Dan… like… like a scarf. Yes! Solved! I wanted to inform Fiona of the situation, so phoned her up there and then (late on a Sunday night) and made the suggestion. She approved of the idea but said, "Dan always wore a hoodie. Could it be a hoodie?"

… and that is how the iconic idea of the hoodie emerged… from a solution to a potentially catastrophic problem! Fiona also said that she thought it would be better for them not to have to see one person playing Dan.

It slowed our rehearsals down but gave them a new focus. We delayed the performance to the family and friends, but everyone understood why. I was so excited and felt it could become the iconic idea from the production!

Amy Sturrock (Megan in the original OYT production – Year 12): I was hastily dismissive about the hoodie idea after Harry left, but that was more due to the fact that I couldn't understand the symbolism. Once I saw it in action it was so apparent that now we could never do the play without it.

Alysha-Jade Patis (Connie in the original OYT production – Year 11): When Harry (Dan) left the cast I remember thinking 'What are we going to do now?' It was late on in the process to bring someone new in, but at the same time Dan is the centre of it. How do we even have a play without a Dan? The hoodie became Dan. Whoever wore the hoodie represented Dan. The hoodie symbolising Dan was such an amazing concept to show everyone had a part of Dan in them and they were also a part of him… and Dan could be anyone.

Sally Britton (Hope in the original OYT production – Year 12): Things seemed very bleak after Harry left. We had worked for so long with him being the centre of our piece and to not have a Dan felt hollow. However, it proved to be the biggest turning point, making it unique. It was not fair to cast someone else as Dan, as we had worked so closely with the family and no-one else seemed right for the role. When we started throwing the hoodie around, or cradling it like a baby, or smelling it, or wearing it like a girlfriend would to her boyfriend's hoodie, or using it as a goal post in football, it felt a lot more personal and the idea took off.

Emily Moulsdale (Kate in the original OYT production – Year 13): I loved the idea of the symbolic hoodie. It enabled us to show different sides to Dan at different times of his life, and helped his friends and family when watching the production as there wasn't just one person portraying Dan.

Carley Sefton-Wilson (Assistant Director, OYT): Losing a central cast member is always really hard, and Harry leaving felt like a big step back to me at the time. The first time I saw the use of the hoodie I knew that's how we had to do it. It was not without challenges, and the cast took a while to develop the idea, but it made the play better. As always, there's a lot to be learned when things go wrong. Harry leaving felt like something so detrimental that it could have affected the whole production, but it ended up being one of the things that made our production work so well.

Chelsea Fisher (Bridget in the original OYT production – Year 12): Dan's home videos and photos tied in beautifully with not having one person playing Dan. The audience was able to see the real Dan. Even through photos, videos and stories told by others, they could see Dan was naturally charismatic and lovable, and that really shone through.

Chapter 13

COSTUME

Kat Chivers (Costume designer for the original OYT production): I had been working with OYT since the 2005 production of *Sequined Suits and Platform Boots*. Previous to that I'd worked with either adult groups, who had a very set idea of what they wanted the costumes to look like, and weren't keen to listen to other ideas, or school plays where a lot was decided by the limited budget. OYT worked differently as everyone had a say and no one was too small to have an input. I always liked that everyone was there 'for the fun of doing it seriously', and that people wore what I gave them without (too much) fuss, even when the costumes were ridiculous ☺

I remember the set and multimedia arriving and thinking they were so much more impressive and impactful than the costumes, but I didn't feel that over-the-top, obvious costumes were right for this story. It was more of a play where the acting needed to draw the audience rather than flashy costumes. I wanted to define the family so they were easily identifiable from the rest of the cast but to keep the costumes subtle. Having an ensemble cast meant t-shirts were the obvious choice to allow people to play different roles without confusing the audience. The DSMF logo was the only real choice to 'decorate' the (black) polo-shirt; anything else would have distracted from the story. I do remember having a debate with the cast about whether polo shirts or round neck t-shirts were better!

The hoodie gave an almost haunting presence, a constant reminder that Dan was no longer here. My main concern with the family costumes was finding clothes that could be multi-functional – look fitting for the funeral scenes but also suitable for the early scenes. I didn't want to have any costume changes as it would interrupt the flow of the performance. I already had the costume for Fiona in mind before I spoke to the cast, but James (Tim), Olivia (Caroline) and Joe (Jacob) were asked to bring something in that they would choose to wear to a special family meal out (that didn't have bright colours or glitter/sparkles). I was keen not to have them all in black as I wanted them to stand out from the ensemble but not in a showy way. They all were brilliant in their choices of shirts/tops and we paired them with black jeans or trousers for the most part. Jacob was the easiest to costume as he had quite a distinct style so it seemed in keeping to stick with that. Fiona's costume was a skirt/dress suit so there was the option to remove the jacket for different scenes if needed. We kept make up to a minimum and hairstyles pulled back from the face to allow clearer voice projection.

Chelsea Fisher (Bridget in the original OYT production – Year 12): The costume is my favourite part of the design of the play. It had never felt right seeing one person as Dan (in both plays). He felt too present in a play that mourned every part of him not being present any more. Mark had the brilliant idea to have everyone play Dan. We showed this using costume. Everybody wore a black polo shirt with the Dan Spargo-Mabbs Foundation logo on the front, but when playing Dan, you'd wear the blue hoodie representing him. This was such a great way of having Dan in the play, but highlighting the feeling of him being so immensely missed.

Chapter 14

AUDIENCE OF FAMILY AND FRIENDS

The delayed performance for family and friends was much anticipated and was only a few weeks before the first public performances. Our Academy had just undergone an Ofsted (or a 'Mocksted') inspection and I remember turning to Paul Ibbott (our composer/musical director and my friend, who had similar reservations about these ridiculous judgements) at the end of the quite incredible performance and I said to him: "How would you grade that then?" He laughed. It was so obviously beyond a grade. Our young people were involved in something that wasn't 'practice' for the real world… this was the real world!

Lewis Evans (Jack in the original OYT production – Year 12): During one of my monologues as Jack, I happened to make eye contact with the real-life Jack, and I remember he mouthed the line I was saying along with me… a moment I will never forget! When we had finished the play, I shyly approached him and the first thing he did; he gave me a hug. That meant more than anything.

Jack: My first viewing was a dress rehearsal in Southampton. It was a remarkably difficult experience and one of the only times I have cried in front of my friends. The talent of the cast was particularly impressive, and the use of a hoodie to represent Dan's identity was quite lovely.

Lewis Evans (Jack in the original OYT production – Year 12): At that time I was really struggling with the relationship I had with my own mother. During the show you have such high adrenaline that you don't pay attention to who is in the audience and just worry about getting through it. I remember vividly for my very last monologue, about being honest with your mother and how those relationships matter, I knelt down, and the first person I saw on the front row was my mother, who I hadn't had contact with for roughly one to two years. I performed the entire monologue, making eye contact with her, as it was the only way I could communicate what and how I was feeling. Powerful beyond measure for myself.

George Davis (Harvey in the original OYT production – Year 11): I thought Natascha played Fiona extremely well and portrayed her perfectly. It was very emotional to sit through, especially sat with Dan's family and other close school friends of mine like Jack.

Bethany: A video of Dan as a baby was shown at the end, with friend/ family photos shown throughout, and it hit all the emotions hard. We were all sat in the room together watching this amazing performance, but the reason for the performance was the worst. I remember thinking how the performers could not have been chosen better. They had all made the effort to really connect with their role and get to know who Dan was. They were so lovely towards us, and I remember them coming up to us all to give us all hugs at the end.

Connie: It was difficult to watch that first time and to see our history literally being acted out in front of our eyes. I thought it was very delicately put together and certainly highlighted the message: know the potential consequences and think about the effects that even one decision could have on both you and all of your loved ones.

Izzy Forrester: I was hugely moved by the performance and the sensitivity of the young actors. Fiona and Tim were at the performance, which made it enormously poignant for me, and I was very aware of wanting to support them. The contributors I talked to are universally proud that they have been part of such a powerful legacy.

Jacob Spargo-Mabbs: The first (and I think only) time I saw the play was a rehearsal of the first Oasis Youth Theatre production directed by Mark. I thought it was very moving and creative. I hadn't realised how much scope for creativity there was with a play taken completely from other people's words.

Tim Spargo-Mabbs: I recall that was the first time I saw 'Dan' collapsing from taking the MDMA and it was like a cold knife going through my heart. This was the only point at which I felt negative emotions. It was funny hearing the words I'd struggled to find for the interviews being recycled in other places and finding they'd stood up rather well, much to my surprise. I loved the performance and finding out where the original cast lived and the landscapes they inhabited. It was lovely.

Sally Britton (Hope in the original OYT production – Year 12): I remember the first showing to Fiona and Tim. Fiona had to leave at one stage. It was overwhelming for all of us as we really felt part of

Dan's life. I realised Natascha, playing Fiona, was particularly similar to Fiona in real life with her physicality and looks and was perfect casting. Then Fiona told me I looked and acted similar to Hope, especially in the silly facial expressions I made which really hit home how real this situation is. I remember her talking about where Dan's resting place was, under a sycamore tree.

Carley Sefton-Wilson (Assistant Director, OYT): I hope Fiona doesn't mind me sharing this. When she first watched the play, in the scene in the hospital when Dan died, it became too much for her and she had to leave the theatre. I took her to one of the side rooms and she became hysterical. It felt like I was watching her relive the most awful moment of her life again. It felt totally helpless to see somebody suffer such pain. What do you say? Normally there would be a longer period of time before anyone is allowed this access following such a tragic event, but at that moment I realised we were part of their grief and of their healing process. I wondered, when I went home that night, whether we were doing the right thing. Tim and Fiona were only beginning to come to terms with what had happened to them, let alone allowing us to make a play about it, but I understood that in their grief, and because of their faith, they just wanted to stop anyone else going through something like this, and so we had to support them. I hope I never know what it's like to lose a child, but in that room with Fiona on that evening, I had an insight into what that pain must feel like. They say there's no word to describe somebody who's lost a child. We have 'widow' for someone who has lost her husband and 'orphan' for someone who has lost their parents. Apparently, this is because no word could ever be found to describe that pain. Seeing Fiona that night relive Dan's death, I understand why.

Fiona Spargo-Mabbs: By the time we saw the first full performance we were familiar with much of it, but that didn't help me cope with seeing it any better. It's an incredible play, and the OYT cast played it so incredibly well, but it was (and still is) too hard for me to watch. There were a few preview performances in Southampton and then the premiere in Croydon, and I watched every one, every time thinking it would get a bit less painful, but it didn't. It just got worse. I've made myself a promise never to watch it again. I break this from time to time, and always, always regret it.

Chapter 15

PUBLIC PERFORMANCES/PREMIERE

Our achievement was as much about 'stickability' as ability. We stuck around and completed our work on the play and performed it. There were times for a few of the cast who thought about jacking it in. For different reason they chose to stick around, and on the first performances I saw the fruits of our labour, and was genuinely proud of the beautiful work we had created from this dreadful experience our new friends had been compelled to live through. I consider myself to be highly fortunate to be surrounded by such able people (adults and young people) who helped me realise this vision and bring about something from nothing – and with no template as to how it should be done. No professional company would get an 18-month preparation period like we had. No small-scale professional company could afford the wealth of talent that we had in OYT working voluntarily. I consider myself supremely fortunate to have the opportunity to head up this achievement.

Alysha-Jade Patis (Connie in the original OYT production – Year 11): I don't remember any single performance but, when I've had to perform a piece over and over again I tend to get bored of it or it loses its meaning or it doesn't seem to have the same effect in later performances. Whenever we performed *ILYMIPIWD* it felt like we were performing it for the first time. All the emotions were raw and we were still exploring the best way to perform it. My family thought it was amazing.

Natascha Thomas (Fiona in the original OYT production): I remember the initial performances; the truth, the relevance, the fact it had happened so soon after the real event and that we had managed to get this together. I couldn't say the audience was going to enjoy *ILYMIPIWD*, I didn't want them to 'have a good time'; I wanted the audience to learn, to be moved, to remember *ILYMIPIWD* and to leave talking about it. I wanted it to make an impact and I know it did! There was not a dry eye in the house, including mine by the time the first performance was over. I knew our emotion, time and determination had been worthwhile! I couldn't console my mum for a little while afterwards, her tears lingering a while after the performance finished, and she knew all of the goings on after each rehearsal but still reacted so emotionally.

My work colleagues said it made them want to go home and hold their children and put them in bubble wrap.

Chelsea Fisher (Bridget in the original OYT production – Year 12): In the final scene of the second Act, *I Promise I Won't Die*, it felt as if it stopped being a play for the last few minutes as we lined up and presented flowers for Dan on the stage for him. I never considered myself to be in role for that final scene. It felt like this was our way to show love and respect for him and his family. We felt so connected to him even though we had never met. I will always be glad that we had a chance to show how loved Dan was by the people that knew him, but also to show we as a cast had love for him too.

Lee Fisher (Parent of cast member): I need to say how gripping *ILYMIPIWD* was. We have lived an experience from the damage of teenage drug use for the last 9 years. My son took drugs, unbeknown to us, from the age of 13, whilst playing football, swimming and boxing. At the age of 16 he was diagnosed with an extreme case of drug-induced psychosis, that developed into severe schizophrenia that he will suffer with for the rest of his life. It has been a long, painful 9 years. This play must be performed to schools, clubs and prisons. People think this won't happen to them or anyone close to them, but it does happen far too often, and it is real.

Kathryn Shotter (College student): It was a moving/tragic story told with elegance and simplicity. I have never clapped so much and cried with pride seeing so many of my lovely friends doing such an excellent job.

Ali Garner (Parent of teenager and teaching assistant): I was deeply moved by *ILYMIPIWD* and the audience reaction to it. It felt like we all had something in common, remembering a loved one we had all lost. It didn't feel like a play about taking illegal substances but a play about loss and relationships. As a mum of a 12-year-old daughter, I am at the stage of allowing her more independence and freedom. She shows many of the traits Dan had and, like him, she is a risk-taker. It brought home to me that it can happen to anyone and any family. I must trust my parental instinct when something doesn't feel quite right, and check things out to make sure to talk openly to her about good and bad risk taking. It dispelled the belief that young people who use drugs are from troubled and disaffected backgrounds, which allows parents to be complacent about their own children and drug-taking. The peer pressure Dan's friend, Jack, faced stood out for me; how he felt responsible for everyone, as he was sober, and how upset he was when not owning up to being at the rave. He was the one person trying to do the right thing. It is so sad he feels he should have done more.

We were delighted to get early reactions from drama teachers who had seen this preview. Their reactions gave an early (not entirely surprising) indication that the play should achieve popularity in drama classrooms.

Alice Mitchell: (Drama teacher from Wiltshire): I haven't stopped thinking about it all day. Beautiful, heart-breaking and truly important. I have never seen a piece of theatre like it. The kids are so affected by *Too Much Punch*: the impact of this new play blows that out of the water. It's a Drama teacher's dream. If you get a chance, go and watch. I promise you, you will want to teach it.

Lisa Gilmour (Drama Teacher from Romsey Hanmpshire): Emotive but also thought-provoking – expertly and authentically performed. It is beautifully crafted with a mix of high energy physical theatre and heart-wrenching, 'talking head' style monologues.

The Entertainment page of our newspaper was equally enthusiastic in their review.

Karen Robson (Southern Daily Echo): A clear-sighted, sobering dramatisation of the facts. The first part of the play was presented with colour, movement and vitality, that perfectly captured the energy of the youthful characters. In contrast, the second was more stately and less showy in the staging, enhancing the general impact and sense of loss. Effortless from this talented cast.

A lot of thought was put into where the official premiere should be held. Dan's school was the first idea but eventually we settled on the prestige of the BRIT School in Dan's home town, Croydon. It made an incredible climax for OYT's work and a performance all the cast remember with much affection.

Natascha Thomas: (Fiona in the original OYT production): I still have 'performing on stage at the BRIT School' on my CV under Key Achievements to this day! An amazing experience!

Emily Moulsdale (Kate in the original OYT production – Year 13): Our most memorable performance was at the BRIT School where a lot of Dan's friends and family attended. Hearing their feedback and knowing they loved what we had created was honouring. When talking of my time in OYT, *ILYMIPIWD* is always the play my family remember most vividly, which pleases me as that is what we aimed to do; tell Dan's story in a way that caused people to think and make different choices, or have a different perspective on life, even years after watching the production!

Ollie Webb (Ensemble in the original OYT production, boy on the cover of the script – Year 8): My favourite performance was at the BRIT school. It felt good to be near the family's home town and perform in such a prestigious venue. Wanting to go into the performing arts, being at the BRIT School on a stage where many other amazing performers had trained was an amazing opportunity. Even though I knew the script, the scene about the funeral, and the lovely words Tim says, always made me tear up. I always felt drained after every performance. It was an emotional rollercoaster. We always wanted to tell Dan's story as best as we could.

Hope: It was tough to watch and there were a lot of details about the night in question that were hard to swallow. I think it made me look differently at certain people. It was hard seeing the video of us (Dan and I) singing and playing guitar. It was raw, which is beneficial to those it was aimed at.

The BRIT School attracted more professional reviews…

Ray Oudkerk (Assistant Principal, BRIT School Performing Arts): I was deeply moved by the play… fascinating for their actuality, honesty, matter-of-factness at times and such impact at others. Informative, complex and subtle – real life on stage. Such an important story to be told. We want our young people to hear it.

I am always particularly thrilled for our 'normal' comprehensive school cast members (and me) to get such enthusiastic praise from institutions we hold in such high esteem.

Paul Webster (Performing Arts and Drama Subject Advisor, Pearson UK): There were many poignant lines so it demonstrated how powerful verbatim theatre can be in capturing 'truth'. I appreciated the play isn't fixated with one message. I hope there are more opportunities for people (and not just young people) to experience this work in the future. Mark has a strong reputation for creating plays that are highly accessible to young people – to perform and to understand – and I hope this will be just as successful.

Peter Graystone (Church Times): The plays are overwhelming. Mark Wheeller has created something remarkable and lasting.

Gareth Davies (Senior Reporter, Croydon Advertiser): I thought the plays were wonderful (if somewhat difficult to watch at times). The verbatim style creates an authenticity and relatability that will prove effective with the target audience. The honesty and frankness of Daniel's friends will help too. I was particularly impressed with the vivid creation of the rave itself. Having been to events like that in the past, the way it was presented, helped by Jack's music, captured what it's like to be there. After I left, my partner picked me up and the first thing I did was to hug my son.

Matt Hobbs (professional actor/singer): I have never been emotionally moved to the extent I was last night, by ANY performance, professional, amateur or youth. To deal with such an emotionally raw piece of text with such dignity was awe-inspiring to watch. I have ZERO recollection of any drug education at school. If watching this play has taught me anything, it's that you need performances like this in schools. You need actual human beings with real life experience around these drugs to talk about their experiences.

I could have added many more reviews echoing the same positive reactions and the recurring idea that 'this play has to be seen in schools'.

Chapter 16

'ILYMIPIWD'... LEGACY

ILYMIPIWD (albeit a shorter – 50 minute – TIE version) is now an established UK touring production originally by Stopwatch and now both Wizard and Tie It Up Theatre Companies. TiU have also, funded by DSMF, produced a high quality virtual (filmed) production. It has become a text schools study and perform having been licensed 545 times in the six years it has been available; nearly 100 performances per year, which includes the pandemic year when live theatre didn't happen. It must now be one of the most popular school texts/performances and reminds me of the popularity *Too Much Punch For Judy* experienced when it was first published. There is much for it yet to achieve. It hasn't taken off internationally but I feel hopeful this will happen. None of us wanted what happened to Dan to have happened but everyone is trying to make the best from the awfulness of his tragedy.

Carley Sefton-Wilson (Assistant Director, OYT): I have lost count of the amount of times I saw this play and I have cried every time. We hoped it would be used in schools as a drug education programme, so it had to be engaging, honest, entertaining and to tell the story well. I remember in one performance, a teacher from the school whose own daughter had died was overwhelmed. I spoke to him afterwards and he said it was the details around the things that no one thinks of that brought it all back again, like organising a funeral for your child, what do you wear?, how do you tell people? He said he wished he could have left the theatre and not watched it as it was like reliving it all again. Even though that was very hard to hear and I felt awful that he was so upset, it made me realise we'd got it right.

The Venerable Christopher Skilton (Archdeacon of Croydon, Anglican Diocese of Southwark – on the professional StopWatch production showcased at Southwark Cathedral): Deeply moving and poignant and so superbly done. Searing honesty, which stems from the fact it captures and uses verbatim accounts so brilliantly. Another part of its strength is that, whilst it does say something about the insidious power of drug culture, it is quite naturally also about friendship, loyalty, parenthood, friendship, trust, identity, family, peer pressure and much more – all woven into a powerful story. Its educational value and potential is enormous.

At the showcase performance I remember thinking this was a 'proper play' in a way I'd never truly allowed myself to believe before. It was in all ways professional. The audience clearly felt the same. They gave it a standing ovation that went on… and on… and on. I rarely use the word 'awesome'… but this was. I felt so proud of what I and OYT had started and then StopWatch under the guiding hand of my friend, (since 1990 when his company StopWatch first took on the rights to tour *Hard to Swallow* and then with incredible success *Chicken*), Adrian New, had built upon so harmoniously.

Connie: I feel oddly proud of Dan. I remember the wonderful person he was – the caring, bright, ambitious and funny person who used to drive me crazy during German lessons, and who we used to prank call in the early hours of the morning at sleepovers. And now he's achieved so much even though he's no longer with us. I think it's extraordinary how far this play has come since the idea was first put forward, and that's credit to Mark and all the talented actors who contributed to it. The idea that it is now to be a set text for Drama GCSE and Dan's story and voice will live on is quite overwhelming.

Izzy Forrester: For me, the most powerful performance experience of the play was with my GCSE Drama group who saw the professional launch at Southwark Cathedral. They were an incredibly talented group, who were particularly inspired by physical theatre and worked organically together. They performed scenes from the play for their exam. Their performances were so moving and brought me to tears on many occasions! I could not have premiered the play at our school. It would have been too emotionally difficult. I remain so grateful OYT for their respectful work with the play and for their contribution to the early days of the Foundation.

George: My partner works in a school and came home saying her students are studying it in Drama. I was shocked and pleased how far the charity and the play has come.

Ollie Webb (Ensemble in the original OYT production, boy on the cover of the script – Year 8): *ILYMIPIWD* hit me hard… but in a good way, if that makes sense. Being so young (11-13) meant I had no previous 'experience' in any of the themes within the play, but it meant I was able to learn about them and educate myself through somebody else's tragedy. This sounds selfish but I would 100% say going through that process has allowed me to have a different and better outlook on life. I've spent a lot of time recently worrying about whether my choices (career, university etc.) are right. When you sent me these questions, and I had the opportunity to look back on it all, it made me realise, I need to stop worrying because life is too short.

I am proud to have my name attached to this play in such a prominent manner and am also thrilled that, as a result of this book, the OYT team can also be accorded due recognition. Without their 'stickability' and creative input the play would have been good but never so 'complete'. I have plays emerging as 'popular' across my career which shows, I believe, sustained 'quality' regarding my own creative output. I guess this led in part to the trust Fiona, her family and Dan's friends showed in me (and OYT) by allowing us to make this play. I remain forever grateful to all those across the years who have trusted me with their words.

Fiona Spargo-Mabbs: We commissioned the play as part of the work of our drug education charity to support young people to make safer choices about drugs. There's something about drama that engages the imagination in a way that nothing else can, and gets into young people's heads and hearts. As a play, young people not only have the opportunity to see a performance, but also to perform it themselves, and to study it in drama lessons, all of which enables them to explore character, and motivation, and reflect on their own perceptions of risk and consequence, and the impact of their decisions on themselves and so many others – all that rehearsal for life stuff that's so important. I don't think this would have worked so well if it wasn't a verbatim play. There's such a power to a play that's not only a true story, but one in which every word was originally spoken by a real person, especially when many of those are the ages of the teenage actors and audiences. I think a dramatisation of what happened to Dan, however well written, could only ever have had just a fraction of the impact *ILYMIPIWD* does.

Tim Spargo-Mabbs: Narratives have their own particular authority, although we as a society are not used to discerning authority like that. Epics like *The Iliad* have one sort of tribal authority, plays have another, more social authority. Individuals learn more about the Holocaust from *The Diary of Ann Frank* and the *Kindness* of Susan Pollack than we do from statistics about '6 million Jews'. Similarly, the sequence of Dan's story lends an authority to lessons about ethics that we would otherwise draw in abstract and from a text book. 'The word became flesh' as the apostle John put it, 'and dwelt among us'.

Fiona Spargo-Mabbs: With the play having toured so extensively now, so many friends have seen it, and everyone is always knocked sideways by it, especially with knowing me, and sometimes also having known Dan. It's an emotional watch at the best of times, and so much more if the story is one you've touched yourself. One anecdote stuck with me because I found it both touching and funny. One of my friends, who I'd known since before Dan was born, and whose children and mine spent lots of time together when they were small, brought her daughter, Beth, to see a performance. Afterwards Beth said, "You know there's a bit in the play where you talk about Dan having put snails in his mouth when he was tiny? Well, Dan used to try to get me to put snails in my mouth in your garden too".

I could just picture these two tiny toddlers, negotiating snail-related experiences in our back garden.

I try to avoid seeing performances now, but every so often there's a new one I need to see. The first touring production with StopWatch, because we'd commissioned this and were funding it at great expense to go into schools, so I needed to see what students were seeing; then the second version when Wizard Theatre took it over in 2020; and the new production with TiU Theatre, also in 2020; and the filmed version of this – for the same reasons. These professional productions have been incredibly well performed, and imaginatively produced, and impossible to watch without being affected and paying a heavy emotional price. I fall right back down the rabbit holes that are always waiting for me anyway all over the place, into those worst of worst times, and into how that felt. I prefer the longer version over the touring one, hard though I find any version to watch. I was sad that Jacob had to be lost in the shortened, touring version, along with other important people like Jenna's mum, Kate, and her brother, Archie. It also loses the scene where Tim and I talk about the dealer, amongst others, along with the two-part structure which I feel works so well, where the first part moves forward, and the second back to little Dan and where he began, and the very different dynamics those two parts have which balance and complement each other so beautifully.

The last time I broke my promise – apart from the touring productions – was at the Edinburgh Fringe in 2018, to which a youth theatre from Yorkshire had taken a production. Tim and I had gone up there to support this, as had Mark and his wife, and we got to know the young people and wider cast and team, and as always quickly grew so fond of them all. They got fantastic five-star reviews, Mark (as always!) worked to persuade me I needed to see it, and I have to confess I was drawn to do so and, on the last night I went. They had adults playing Tim and me, and one other person, and teenagers playing the teenagers, and it was incredible. But also so, so hard to watch – as always. Like nothing else does, it takes me right back to those moments, and makes it all far too real again.

Tim Spargo-Mabbs: I also prefer the longer version of the play – it is more complete and satisfying. I loved an immersive performance of the full version at a college in 2019. For the first half hour we were all in a rave mingling with teens, dealers and police. It reinforced the narrative authority somehow by saying 'this is (sort of) what it was like where and when Dan died'. It's the nearest I'll ever come to a rave (probably).

Fiona Spargo-Mabbs: I remember at the start saying to Izzy and Tim and others involved in it all and the charity, "Wouldn't it be incredible if it became a set text?"… never really dreaming it would. It will now reach so many more young people in so many more places, with the important messages we hope and pray will protect them from harm. It also gives it a credibility which will last beyond its term as a set text, which means it's more likely to be chosen by drama teachers and continue to reach more young people. Dan would be so chuffed to see his story right there next to Shakespeare and JB Priestly, though we'd all, of course – Dan most of all, of course – prefer his story wasn't there to be told.

Jacob Spargo Mabbs: Becoming a set text is an exciting opportunity. It's a testament to Mark's ability to turn the inarticulate words of deeply hurt people into a beautiful, moving and evocative piece of theatre. It also feels like a vindication of the motives of the Foundation in creating the play.

Fiona Spargo-Mabbs: Thank you so much, Mark and OYT, for creating this beautiful piece of theatre, for us and for Dan. Whatever happens to us, and to the charity, this play will be there as the best possible legacy for a boy who loved nothing more than hanging around in the drama studio, messing about in the costume cupboard, entertaining the world around him, and bringing so much energy, life and joy to so many.

The End

OYT Contributors:
Where Are They Now?

Sadly, OYT is no more.

Its value was overwhelmingly obvious. It offered aspirations for its members (a core value of any educational institution) but attracted intake over the years because of its high regard and reputation. It also assisted with academic results; those in OYT achieved well in examinations because they were in a pattern of committing and achieving and felt particularly good about themselves.

In 2022, long after I left in 2018, a small group of Year 10 students from Oasis Academy, Lordshill, performed an extract from *Too Much Punch For Judy*. I have no idea whether any connection was made between the origins of my plays and the Academy these students attend but I hope it was.

I remain grateful to the support Oasis gave me for nine successful and productive years. OYT's legacy is assured through many of our productions which are now available for others to watch and perform.

OYT's legacy is most effectively secured through the lives and achievements of its alumni. Here's a snapshot of what the group who contributed to this book are doing some five years after the production:

Sally Britton (Hope in the original OYT production): Since *ILYMIPIWD* I moved to London and have worked on new writing, short films, and was a member of the Youth Board for the Royal Court Theatre, London. I travelled Asia and Australia, which inspired me to start writing. I am currently studying acting at The Liverpool Institute of Performing Arts. Acting, and particularly devising, is a huge passion for me. OYT will always hold a place in my heart – along with this piece of theatre. I am so privileged to be a part of it.

George Davis (Harvey in the original OYT production): After *ILYMIPIWD* I performed in another of Mark's plays, *This Is For You*. OYT was disbanded but I followed Mark to help make Romsey School Community Youth Theatre (RSCoYT). I went from one of the youngest in OYT, to one of the oldest in RSCoYT. I had a leadership role within the cast. We performed *Butcher, Butcher, Burning Bright* and *Can You Hear Me Major Tom?* at RSCOYT. I attended university for a year studying acting.

Although I really enjoyed my time there, I ended up choosing to work and am now under RPS Group for Bournemouth Water, finding water leaks and reducing water wastage. OYT helped me massively and gave me the ability to work well in a team, especially under stressful conditions.

Lewis Evans: (Jack in the original OYT production): OYT was the foundation of why and how I'm now an actor. It gave me a creative platform as we were able to thrive by curating as well as be actors. I was cast by StopWatch Theatre Company for the second professional touring version of *ILYMIPIWD* as Jack (again!), my first professional acting job, bringing a bitter-sweet end to my involvement with *ILYMIPIWD*. I spent a year touring Germany as part of another professional TIE company. For the last 3 years I have been working in TV and film. At the time of writing, I'm an actor on the set of *Ted Lasso*. I am also the co-founder of Box House Theatre who, in 2022, presented an original (platform theatre) play *Twisted Tales* at the Camden Fringe (also touring schools). There is no way I'd be doing any of this without OYT.

Chelsea Fisher (Bridget in the original OYT production): I continued to be a part of Youth Theatre, joining OYT 006 (a branch of OYT where members work more independently) and created an original piece that was taken around the country in drama festivals, winning prizes. I am now a drama coach for younger children. Spending so much time in OYT is still valuable when it comes to how I run my clubs, ensuring everyone feels heard, and allowing them to be creative and free with the work they do. I feel extremely honoured to have been a part of *ILYMIPIWD* from the beginning, and hope it continues to teach and inspire others.

Emily Moulsdale (Kate in the original OYT production): OYT taught me so much more than how to perform on a stage, from communication to working as a part of a team, and it gave me so much confidence in so many aspects of my life. Being a part of *ILYMIPIWD* helped me on many occasions in my career now as a paediatric nurse – from guiding parents though the loss of their child to caring for patients who have suffered from drug-induced illness. I feel I would not be able to empathise with these individuals in the way that I do, had I not been a part of *ILYMIPIWD*.

Alysha-Jade Patis (Connie in the original OYT production): Being part of OYT made me discover how much I loved drama and how it can move and change people. I love not only the confidence it gave me onstage but in myself to lead others. I stayed with OYT for a while, not just as cast but as an Assistant Director in later projects, most notably *Can You Hear Me Major Tom?*. I took Performing Arts at College and studied acting at university. I am still inspired by the way we all worked together and the fact that it was a safe space that allowed us to make mistakes without the fear of failure. Nothing was ever 'wrong', nobody was ever judgmental, and nothing was impossible. I cherish my time at OYT. It kick-started my love for theatre.

Amy Sturrock (Megan in the original OYT production): *ILYMIPIWD* was my final OYT project. I'd focused on college and growing through the remainder of my teenage years. OYT gave me a confidence I never thought I'd have. I spent a lot of my years at OYT, made amazing friendships and found a talent and passion I didn't know I had. It was worth every minute and I'm forever glad I did it.

Natascha Thomas: (Fiona in the original OYT production): I was a member of OYT for nine years. I still mention it a lot in my day to day life. In interviews I discuss OYT for a while. I worked as a travel rep overseas, and delivered meetings to 40-200 people daily. Had I not been on stage with OYT I feel as though I may not have been as successful in this role! Most of the best things that happened in my school and college years were with OYT. I made friends, memories, trips, and had experiences that will last a lifetime!

Ollie Webb (Ensemble in the original OYT production, boy on the cover of the script): After *ILYMIPIWD*, I did *This Is For You* with OYT. I achieved GCSE Dance grade 7. I went on to Richard Taunton's Sixth Form College to gain a triple Distinction in the Level 3 National Extended Diploma in Performing Arts (Musical Theatre), and a Distinction in the Level 3 Subsidiary Diploma in Dance. I am currently on a gap year and looking to take Contemporary Dance at degree level. I am part of three dance companies: ZoieLogic Dance Theatre, a Southampton-based dance/theatre company which challenges the perceptions of dance; and I work as a freelance dancer in FuzzyLogic, one of the UK's leading youth companies and ORB Male Youth Dance Company, a contemporary dance/theatre company run by the Luke Brown Company in partnership with The Point, Eastleigh.

Digital Resources for Teachers

A DVD of the full original production is also available – please see the Teaching Resources page on www.salamanderstreet.com for further details.

I Love You, Mum – I Promise I Won't Die DVD

By Oasis Youth Theatre, directed by Mark Wheeller.

"OYT worked as an amazing ensemble but stand out performances came from Lewis Evans and Natasha Thomas who took on the roles of Dan's best friend and Dan's mum respectively with such ease. The set was simple with 6 cubes moved around at pace to create new scenes and also used in slow motion during the opening rave scene to great effect; flying around the stage with the chemical formula for MDMA projected upstage certainly marked the moment. The upstage screens also projected text message conversations and photographs of Dan throughout which disintegrated into flying sycamore seeds – symbolic of growing goodness from such sadness. At the end of such an amazing performance you would typically expect a standing ovation but this was so emotionally draining you felt too numb to stand." Holly Barradell – Ink Pellet

More information about the play can be found on Mark's YouTube Channel (and do please subscribe for all the latest updates) where there is a specific *ILYIPIWD* playlist to support teachers: https://www.youtube.com/c/MarkWheeller

Mark Wheeller on Twitter **@MarkWheeller**

The script for *I Love You Mum – I Promise I Won't Die* is available from Methuen: https://www.bloomsbury.com/uk/i-love-you-mum--i-promise-i-wont-die-9781350011281/

The Daniel Spargo-Mabbs Foundation

The Daniel Spargo-Mabbs Foundation is a drug education charity providing a range of evidence-based resources and support for schools, colleges and community organisations across the UK:

- **Interactive drug education workshops for students** (in person and online).

- **A spiral curriculum of evidence-based planning and resources for teachers to deliver drug education in PSHE** for each year group from Year 7 to sixth form. These are available as lessons or adapted as shorter form-time sessions. They are designed to meet the requirements of the statutory Relationships, Sex and Health Education curriculum, and are free to download from the website.

- **Training for teachers and school/college staff** (in person and online).

- **Workshops and webinars for parents and carers** about young people, drugs and decisions (in person and online).

- **A Youth Ambassador programme** to train sixth form students as positive peer influences within their community.

Theatre in Education tours of 'I Love You, Mum – I Promise I Won't Die' are commissioned by the DSM Foundation annually. Professional performances of a shortened version of the play, adapted by Mark Wheeller, are followed by interactive drug education workshops. Drama-based TIE touring productions are also available directly from the licensed TIE companies.

I Wish I'd Known – Young People, Drugs and Decisions: A Guide for Parents and Carers, **Fiona Spargo-Mabbs (Sheldon Press, 2021)** is a handbook for parents and carers which weaves Dan's story around a wealth of information and practical advice. Three sets of supplementary materials to accompany the book are available digitally from the John Murray Learning Library: https://library.johnmurraylearning.com/ebook/I-Wish-I'd-Known/861203

- *Schools, Colleges, Drugs and Decisions – A Pack for Teachers.*

- *Drugs, Decisions and Difference – Neurodiversity and Drug Use in Young People.*

- *Faith, Drugs and Decisions – A Pack for Christian Parents and Faith Leaders.*

All proceeds from book sales go to the DSM Foundation.

For more information about the DSM Foundation see <u>www. dsmfoundation.org.uk</u>

For inquiries about drug education or TIE tours please contact <u>admin@dsmfoundation.org.uk</u>

Scheme of Work

by Annette Hulme

Contents

The Scheme of Work

I have taught *Hard To Swallow* as a set text for some time, and have been fortunate to have Mark Wheeller work with my students for a number of years in the run-up to the written exam. The way in which he has inspired students to move beyond their preconceptions, expand their ideas and use their creativity to approach script, has been a delight to see. There are very few set texts where you have the opportunity to work with the playwright, and I'm so glad I asked Mark, tentatively, all those years ago if he ever did workshops in schools!' *I Love You, Mum – I Promise I Won't Die* is an incredibly powerful play, which moved me to tears the first time I read it: I very quickly decided it was the set text I was going to teach. I was therefore delighted (and surprised!) when Mark asked me to write a scheme of work to accompany this book.

Schemes of work can be challenging to develop, even for your own students: you're making educated guesses at how long tasks will take, how quickly students will engage with a text or a concept, and which tasks will prove challenging, fun or even useful. Writing one for students you've never met, in schools you've never heard of, for teachers you don't know, is particularly interesting! I won't make the grand claim that there is 'something for everyone' here, but I have written the kind of scheme of work I would love to see more of: one that offers a range of approaches, which doesn't assume a particular context (hour-long lessons, a drama studio, access to technology, etc, etc) and which keeps in mind all three of these objectives:

1. To encourage a creative approach to studying and interpreting a set text

2. To look at the play from the perspective of actor, director and designer, and

3. To ensure students are well-prepared for the written exam

Although much of this scheme of work could equally be used to explore the play in preparation for a performance, I wanted all of the activities and tasks to have a direct and purposeful link to the requirements of the Eduqas written exam. Few of us are involved in drama and theatre because we want students to develop a deep love of writing about plays, but just because there is an end goal, it doesn't mean getting to it can't be enjoyable for us or those with whom we work!

After some suggested preparatory tasks for teachers, the scheme of work begins with how to tackle the play initially, and then you will find it organised by particular areas of study. You know your students and your circumstances best, so within each area is a number of possible tasks from which you can choose. Whether you are in a classroom, a drama studio, or anything in between, there are activities you can use wholesale, suggested adaptations, homework and research tasks, group activities, discussion points, practical and written tasks, as well as some 'top tips'. A list of resources is given where required, and at the end of each section is a 'learning checklist', identifying what has been covered and the skills students should have acquired.

I hope this approach gives teachers plenty of ideas, the flexibility to make the teaching of the text your own, and helps to get your students excited about the play and feeling confident ahead of their exams.

Annette Hulme

* If you email Mark, and he's available, he'll make every effort to come into your school or work with your students online. You won't regret it! And, if you have the budget, why not commission your very own Mark Wheeller play?!

Key to the Activities

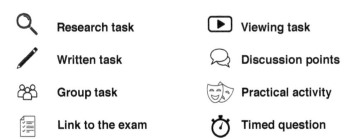

Q	Research task		▶	Viewing task
✎	Written task		💬	Discussion points
👥	Group task		🎭	Practical activity
📋	Link to the exam		⏱	Timed question

Note: The play is in two acts, the first entitled *I Love You, Mum*, the second *I Promise I Won't Die*. Sections are numbered 1-4 in the first act and 1-7 in the second, so it is important students distinguish between the two. Throughout the scheme of work, the play as a whole is abbreviated as *ILYM*; where sections are referenced, they are preceded by *ILYM* or *IPIWD*.

Learning Objectives

The scheme of work equips students to:

- ✓ demonstrate an understanding of the social, historical and cultural context of the play
- ✓ show knowledge and understanding of the original production
- ✓ communicate understanding of verbatim theatre and TIE, and the purpose of such work
- ✓ discuss relevant themes and issues in the play
- ✓ consider the impact of structure
- ✓ show understanding of style, through design and performance
- ✓ write with confidence from the point of view of actor, director and designer
- ✓ explain how design and technical elements can enhance a performance of the play
- ✓ develop individual design concepts
- ✓ explain relevant rehearsal techniques and their application in practice
- ✓ discuss characters and how these can effectively be portrayed to an audience
- ✓ describe how performance techniques can be used to communicate meaning
- ✓ analyse key scenes in detail and with precision
- ✓ use appropriate terminology and vocabulary to describe performance and design elements
- ✓ respond to short-answer and higher-tariff questions, fulfilling the marking criteria
- ✓ manage time effectively under exam conditions

Before You Start:
Tasks for Teachers

Explore the Eduqas website

The Eduqas website is the place to start in order to determine precisely what students need to know for the written exam. There is a wealth of information and numerous resources available on the website. Some key places to look include:

Specification: for Component 3: areas students should cover; structure of the written exam; specific details of texts/their use in the exam. In addition: appendices with drama terminology and rehearsal techniques; under AO2 (for C2, but nonetheless helpful), a list of performance and design techniques

Useful Resources Guide: information on, and links to, a wide range of materials

Eduqas GCSE Drama – How To Mark: a useful PowerPoint walking through how to mark low and higher-tariff questions, with examples

Online Exam Reviews: Component 3 questions, mark schemes and marked responses for previous years

Sample Assessment Materials: exemplar C3 questions

Examiners' Reports

Past Papers

Digital Resources: including Knowledge Organisers, Design Tools and an Exam Walk-Through aimed at learners

Divide the play into extracts*

In the written exam, students will be asked to focus on an extract from the play. This is usually a few pages (in the past, around 2-4). Some time spent dividing the play up into extracts of around 3-5 pages is really helpful. I label them A-Z (or, in the case of *ILYM*, I have done A-P) to avoid confusion with section numbers, put them into a table with section and page references (and start and end points if they're not obvious), with a column next to them for names. You can then use these:

- To set practice questions and papers
- To allocate to individuals, pairs or groups when tackling acting or design questions
- In practical activities
- In research tasks
- To get students used to focusing on a concise section of the set text

Each time you set a task involving a short extract from the play (or a longer one by grouping extracts together), you can assign individuals, pairs or groups, keeping track of who has looked at which sections. The aim of such tasks is to pool resources through feedback to the class, copying and sharing notes, etc, but it is helpful to keep track of who has covered what, ensuring that students don't become 'experts' in one or two extracts, at the expense of a broader overview.

* These are the extracts referred to throughout the scheme of work.

Buy recordings of *I Love You, Mum – I Promise I Won't Die* (*ILYM*)

Get the DVD of Oasis Youth Theatre's (OYT) production of *ILYM*. Not only will it be incredibly helpful for you and your students to see a performance of the play, it will be invaluable when responding to questions asking about the original staging.

If you can, subscribe to the streamed performance of *ILYM* by TiE It Up Theatre. You get a year's access to the production and a detailed Drama Teacher's Resource Pack and Drug Education Resource Pack.

Look at the Daniel Spargo-Mabbs Foundation website

As outlined on p77–78 of this book, there is a great deal of invaluable information on the website, not just about Dan's story. There are many opportunities to tie the teaching and/ or performance of *ILYM* to wider drugs education (including working with the DSM Foundation), and to develop its potential impact beyond the Drama classroom.

Ways In

TOP TIP

Don't begin by watching a production of the play. It will be really useful later on, but at the start it can shut down creativity and lead to students interpreting it as the 'definitive' approach.

RESOURCES

- Class set of *ILYM**
- *Drama Schemes* by Mark Wheeller
- 'Happy Soap' story

* these are not referenced again in Resources

Read-through

I usually begin studying a set text with a read-through, with students taking on roles for a section at a time. *ILYM* is not a lengthy play, so a couple of lessons spent on this can be really helpful in giving students an overview, putting the play in context and beginning to open up discussion about the subject matter, in particular.

'Happy Soap'

If you prefer, one of Mark's schemes of work from *Drama Schemes* offers a more practical alternative to establish a 'way in' via the subject matter. The original story (*The Story of Wacky Soap: A Cautionary Tale* by Mark and Rachel Wheeller) has been re-written by Fiona Spargo-Mabbs as *Happy Soap*, and is due to be published soon. There is also a script based on the original version (published by dbda, 1999), and an edited version of the story in *Drama Schemes*. As the title suggests, the story uses allegory to present a cautionary tale about substance misuse. Although the scheme of work was originally written for Year 7, there are plenty of practical and discussion-based activities to choose from or adapt which, as Mark Wheeller says, allow students to "explore old issues afresh".

LEARNING CHECKLIST

✓   Introduce the set text
✓   Begin to explore the context of the story

Genre & Style

RESOURCES

- Internet access
- NT video: 'An Introduction to Verbatim Theatre'
- NT video: 'The Ethics of Verbatim Theatre'

Defining the genre

Mark Wheeller describes the play as both Verbatim and Theatre In Education (TIE*), "but primarily verbatim". Ask students to research definitions for both: What is TIE? What is Verbatim? Agree and display a 'class definition' for reference.

*A quick word of warning: there is an excellent touring, one-act TIE version of *ILYM*, but the structure is obviously very different (as is the script), so don't use this as the basis for study of the play as a set text!

Understanding verbatim

As a starting point, there is a very good National Theatre video, An Introduction to Verbatim Theatre (available on their YouTube channel), which summarises the genre well. It is around eight minutes long and includes interviews with practitioners including Alecky Blythe (*London Road*) and David Hare (*Stuff Happens*).

Mark Wheeller writes in this book about the sense of responsibility he felt as a playwright telling Dan's story – to do Dan justice, to repay the trust shown in him by Fiona and Tim, and to produce something hard-hitting which didn't overstep the mark. His story in Chapter 1 about the Spanish playwright who initially approached Fiona gives a good indication of how lightly you need to tread when creating a piece of verbatim theatre*. Another of the National Theatre's videos – The Ethics of Verbatim Theatre – provides further helpful insights on this. Both NT videos are well worth watching in class or setting as homework research tasks.

Some points for discussion:

- Why turn Dan's story into a play?
- Why use verbatim? (read what Fiona says about this in Chapter 16)
- Why did Fiona and Tim say yes at all, even to Mark Wheeller, given the pain of watching what Carley Sefton Wilson (Assistant Director, OYT) describes as "the most awful aspects of your life"?
- And finally, what are the responsibilities of those staging, rather than writing, a verbatim play – the directors, actors and designers?

* There is further reference to the ethical issues of both documentary and verbatim theatre in Mark's book *Verbatim: The Fun of Making Theatre Seriously.*

Introduction to verbatim

This is an adaptation of a task Mark Wheeller has used in workshops to explore narrative in theatre*:

- Students should get into pairs (A and B)
- In 30 seconds, A tells B something they did yesterday which is true. (Although not necessary until the 'Time-travelling' task, it saves time if the story selected has another person who was present/around when it took place; they don't need to be important to the story – eg student waking up in the morning; mum in her room)
- B repeats the story back to A as if it is <u>their</u> story (ie in the first person), replicating as much as possible A's speech patterns, mannerisms, facial expressions, gestures, etc
- Swap over, with B telling A their own story
- A repeats the story back to B as if it's their own

An optional extension at this stage is to repeat the same steps as above for the same story, but adding one or more of the following:

- A small, very plausible lie
- A less plausible lie
- A ludicrous lie

Adding lies establishes a further connection to *ILYM* and the different versions of the 'truth' revealed (eg party/rave; first/third time taking drugs), but this is not integral to the task.

Working together in their pairs, focusing on <u>one</u> of their stories (or around 30 seconds of it, if time is short) and with both students playing the <u>same</u> character (ie telling the story between them), the students:

- Experiment with adding movement and gesture to bring the story to life

- Work on ensuring their two versions of the same character are sufficiently alike that the audience sees them as one character. (This focus is a useful tie-in to several members of the ensemble portraying Dan in the play).

Finally, see some or all of the stories.

* There is an extension of this activity in the 'Time-travelling' task in Acting, so you may choose to do both together, or tackle the follow-up fairly soon afterwards

Linking genre to responses

When students are more familiar with the play, revisit the definitions from the 'Defining the genre' task. To get students thinking about how to incorporate references to genre in their responses, ask them to write a sentence connecting each genre to an aspect assessed in the exam:

Eg *ILYM is a verbatim play, so when playing the role of X I would reflect this in my vocal delivery by...*

Eg *As the play has an important TIE message, I would want to highlight this in my set design by…*

Defining the style

In the exam, students will need to describe the style of the play. Mark Wheeller explains in Chapter 1 that the style of the two acts evolved from the structure*. He notes that, much like *Chequered Flags*, a "stylistic contrast" emerged between *ILYM* and *IPIWD*. His explanation, in the TiE It Up! Teacher Resource, is that "some of the scenes are naturalistic whilst other scenes are highly stylised. The whole production style could be described as 'stylised'".

Ollie Webb (ensemble in the original production – and the boy on the cover of the script!) talks in Chapter 8 about the "stylised rave" sequence. Read his description of what that meant to the cast, which clearly conveys what 'stylised' might look like in practice.

Some questions to consider:

- Why might a naturalistic representation of the rave be less effective for an audience?
- What are some other moments or scenes in the play where a stylised approach could work well?

* see Structure for further details.

LEARNING CHECKLIST

✓ Define genre – TIE and verbatim – and connect both to exam responses
✓ Explore verbatim, theoretically and practically
✓ Consider the ethical implications of verbatim theatre
✓ Identify the style of the play

Structure

RESOURCES

* OYT production of *ILYM*

Timeline

Organise the events of the play into a timeline. Either keep it simple or give more detail, referencing where exactly in the two acts each event is discussed. You could begin with Dan's childhood, then his early years at secondary school, sixth form, the first time he took MDMA and so on.

Eg A more detailed timeline, for October/November 2013, might read: *'First time Dan takes MDMA', ILYM, Section 1, p16; IPIWD, Section 7, p65*

Settings summary

Create a simple table* for the two acts, with the section numbers and headings, page numbers and the setting(s) for each. It's a very simple visual way for students to find their way around the text, and is also a very useful resource when beginning to think about set design.

* There is a task in Set Design ('Expanding the settings summary') which uses this table: if it is done on paper, students could helpfully add an additional column at this stage for later use; if it is done on computer and saved, the extra column can be added if/when required

The structure of the play

Mark Wheeller talks in the book about the reasoning behind having two acts (volume of material, primarily!). Look at what he says in Chapter 4 regarding learning about and deciding on structure, the order of the two plays and the reverse telling in *IPIWD**. Some questions to consider:

- What is the impact of Mark Wheeller's decision to split the play as he did?
- *ILYM* is primarily the friends' story; *IPIWD* is the family's:
  - Why did he decide to put the friends' account of the events first?
  - What is the impact of Fiona appearing in the first act (a consequence of her being present when Hope was interviewed)? Why did Mark decide to keep her in the 'friends' play?
  - What is the difference in mood and atmosphere in the two acts?
- Mark says "the audience already knew what had happened to Dan" (we learn from Izzy that he has died right at the beginning of the opening scene of *ILYM*). So, although *ILYM* tells the story mostly chronologically, like *Hard To Swallow*, we are told the tragic outcome very early on. How might that affect the audience response?
- What is the impact of telling the family's story (*IPIWD*) in reverse, especially already knowing the outcome from *ILYM*?

- What is the effect of what Mark Wheeller calls the "circular structure" of the play?

* There is further discussion on the use of structure in this and other plays in Chapter 15 of *Verbatim: The Fun of Making Theatre Seriously*.

Transitions between scenes

One of the structural characteristics of *ILYM* is the seamless movement between present and past, as aspects of the story are referenced or recreated*. This presents challenges for designers and performers (so it is something worth returning to when discussing both design and performance). In *Verbatim: The Fun of Making Theatre Seriously*, Mark Wheeller talks about the decision to ban blackouts from his productions, and the benefit of this "forcing creativity" in the transitions between scenes and sections. Can students identify some of the more challenging moments of transition in the play, for example where it moves a number of times between present and past, or where a completely different setting is required? What are some creative solutions, from design and performance perspectives?

* see also the 'Time-travelling' task in Performance.

Contrasts in the two acts

When students are more familiar with the play and have some of their own ideas, watch the OYT production of *ILYM*. Return to the question of the difference in mood and atmosphere in the two acts. Look at what Karen Robson from the Southern Daily Echo said in her review of the production in Chapter 15. Can students identify how "colour, movement and vitality" were created in *ILYM*? What made the staging in *IPIWD* "more stately and less showy"? And how was a "sense of loss" conveyed?

LEARNING CHECKLIST

- ✓ Produce a timeline and settings summary
- ✓ Understand the structure of the play and how structural decisions alter/create impact
- ✓ Examine the differences in content and mood in the two acts
- ✓ Consider challenges and approaches to transitions in the play

Issues & Themes

RESOURCES

- Internet access
- DSM Foundation website
- Expanded Kübler-Ross Grief Cycle
- *Optionally:* Gagging For It *by Danny Sturrock;* Gail is Dead – *TV documentary film*

Social, historical & cultural context

In the exam, students will be required to show awareness of the social, historical and cultural context of the play. There are a number of useful areas on which to focus: assigning each to several individuals or a small group to research and feed back to the class is an efficient way to cover a lot of ground. I would focus particularly on:

- Rave culture
- MDMA – what it is and the effects; MDMA/Ecstasy

- Laws on possession/supply of drugs (around 2014 and since)
- Other cases of drug overdoses in the media
- Attitudes towards drugs and 'drug culture'
- Jimmy Mizen (the son of Margaret Mizen, whom Fiona references in *IPIWD*, Section 6)
- Media response to Dan's story

If you have a large class, or want to avoid hearing repeats of Google's top search result, you could sub-divide an area: with similar cases you could assign individual stories – eg Leah Betts, Lauren Atkinson, Leah Robinson; for Dan's story split it into immediate response, suppliers being charged, the launch of the DSM Foundation, the trial.

Themes in the play

A useful starting point when exploring themes is to ask, besides the plot, 'What is the play about?' and gather the students' thoughts. Clearly the play will speak differently to different people, but where is there common ground?

To what extent do students agree with the following who describe the themes of *ILYM*: Ali Garner, parent & TA (Chapter 15), The Venerable Christopher Skilton, Archdeacon of Croydon, on the professional StopWatch production (Chapter 16).

Draw up a list of the themes mentioned in these two reviews.

In Chapter 16, although she doesn't refer to it explicitly as a 'theme', Fiona Spargo-Mabbs discusses the concept of 'risk and consequence'. Should this be added to the list? Are there any other themes students would identify, such as responsibility, faith, or grief?

Why do themes matter?

Themes are one aspect of studying plays which can feel a bit 'English essay'. Students are able to identify and tell an examiner 'what the play is about' but, once they know, what do they <u>do</u> with that information? It may seem obvious, but it is worth asking the question: 'Why do we need to know what the themes are?':

- To determine how to tackle the play
- To inform decisions about design – the stage picture, symbolism, colour, etc
- To decide how characters and relationships should be presented
- To dictate the mood and atmosphere – of the whole production and at specific points
- To decide the focus

These are just a few points, and already they cover everything that is and happens on stage!

Ask students to get into groups and either allow them to choose or assign one or two main themes (eg 'risk and consequence'; 'loss'; 'loyalty and responsibility') to each group. They should work their way through the following, ready to feed back to the class:

- What could the audience see in the set design which reinforces your theme(s)?
- Select one key extract/scene from the play where your theme is particularly relevant
  - How might you use projection, lighting and sound to convey your theme?
  - How could costume and props reflect it?
  - How might you use physicality and movement, voice and interaction to highlight it?
- Are there any other ways in which your audience could get a clear message of 'what the play is about'?

Grief

Show students the expanded Kübler-Ross Grief Cycle (which has 7 stages of grief, instead of the original 5: *shock*, denial, anger, depression, bargaining, *testing*, acceptance), and briefly summarise the 7 stages. Which can they see reflected in Dan's family, friends, girlfriend, etc, at specific points in the play?

Focus on one or two brief extracts from the play (eg *ILYM*, Section 4, p33 – Jack's initial reaction to the news; *IPIWD*, Section 2 – the funeral). Can students identify which stages are being exhibited by specific characters? How might each stage manifest itself physically and vocally? Use volunteers and forum theatre to work specifically on how grief might effectively be portrayed in these extracts.

Drugs

There are a number of resources worth exploring to gain a greater understanding of the background to the play; these are just a few of them:

- Daniel Spargo-Mabbs Foundation (www.dsmfoundation.org.uk): an excellent resource – as well as telling Dan's story, there is a huge amount of information and advice about drugs and the law, aimed both at young people and parents. The 'More Information' section also provides links to a number of other websites.
- *Gagging For It*!: a play about anti-social behaviour and the drink/drugs culture in Ibiza, written by Danny Sturrock (lighting and multi-media design for ILYM); available on Amazon
- *Gail is Dead* – the award-winning TV film Mark describes having been shown as a Year 10 student; on YouTube in four parts

LEARNING CHECKLIST

✓ Understand the social, historical and cultural context of the play
✓ Consider the main themes in the play
✓ Explore the connection between themes and directorial approach, design and performance
✓ Consider how a specific theme can be communicated through performance skills

Characters

TOP TIP

Whenever you are looking at an extract, ask students to identify 5-8 key moments – a mixture of lines, actions, reactions, etc. This provides an excellent structural guide and clear focus for written responses.

RESOURCES

- Internet access (or dictionaries/ thesauruses)
- Personality/emotion wheel

Adjectives

When writing about characters, it can be easy to fall into repetitive descriptions, which in turn lead to vague responses: *'To show Fiona feels guilty, I would look guiltily at the ground'*. Finding a range of words to describe a character – particularly at different points in the play – can be a really useful exercise. In *ILYM*, where there is a large group of friends, it's also a helpful way to begin to distinguish individuals. There are a number of ways you could do this, for example:

- Give two or three characters to each student, and ask them to find 5 or 10 adjectives to describe them. If you want them to trace the changes in a character, they could also give example page numbers for each word. Share or compile these words into lists for the whole class to access

- Use a personality or emotion wheel as a starting point (there is a good one at https://www.visualcapitalist. com/a-visual-guide-to-human-emotion/, but Google Images will reveal dozens). Ask students to identify which characters fall where on the wheel and where in the play. Which adjectives apply? Are there others they would add?

Getting to know the characters

There are quite a lot of characters in *ILYM*, so students need to be organised in order to keep track of them and ensure they could write about any of them in an exam. One way to tackle this is to draw up character sheets – one for each character in the play. This is an ideal group task, with each group (of 4-6) taking one or more characters (ideally those connected to each other, for efficiency's sake) and each person in the group looking at 2-4 sections of the play, then discussing and pooling ideas as a group. Once completed, the sheets can be uploaded or copied for sharing with the class.

Areas to consider might include:

- Given circumstances
- Key scenes/moments
- Key lines/speeches
- Character objectives in key sections
- Character super-objective

Beginning character responses

Once they have a wider vocabulary at their disposal and greater understanding of each character, it is much easier for students to explain with focus how a role might be played, or a key moment delivered. Either assign the whole class a specific character, or allow students to choose one on whom they have already focused (if you are assigning a specific one, it's probably fairest to let students know in advance so they can revise from the character sheets above). You can either give them a free choice of which extract (of around 2 pages) they wish to focus on, or assign an extract in advance.

Using their sheets/information gathered in the two tasks above and their own preparation, ask students to respond to a fairly generic question, such as: 'How would you play the role of x in y extract?'. As they may so far have done relatively little work on performance skills specific to the play, you could reduce the scope of the question by asking them to pick just 3 or 4 key moments and/or respond in note form (listing for each key moment how they would use voice, movement and interaction).

LEARNING CHECKLIST

✓ Develop the vocabulary to describe characters effectively
✓ Identify individual characteristics
✓ Use some Stanislavskian approaches to explore character
✓ Begin to apply knowledge of the play to exam-style questions

Rehearsal Techniques

RESOURCES

- Rehearsal techniques worksheet

Rehearsal techniques table

A useful starting point for students is a table of potential rehearsal techniques, with four columns:

- The rehearsal technique
- The definition
- 'Would help with'
- Example (of a character and extract/section where it would be helpful to the actor playing that role)

'Would help with' is particularly useful: students are usually very familiar with techniques such as hot-seating, thought-tracking, and so on, but less adept at knowing when an actor or director might choose to use them as a tool in rehearsal.

I usually produce a worksheet, listing a number of rehearsal techniques in the first column, and a couple of spare lines for additional techniques, then I fill in a couple of cells (definitions and 'would help with') as examples for the students to follow. They can then research for themselves definitions and examples and share with the rest of the class, with a whole-class table produced live in the lesson and shared to all students. If using the whole play is too overwhelming or time-consuming, ask individuals or pairs to focus on an extract or two, a few sections, or one act of the play only.

Alternatively, asking students to complete the table above independently is a helpful homework task, particularly ahead of working on rehearsal techniques in the lesson and/or completing practice questions.

Rehearsal techniques in action

Once students have a good working knowledge of rehearsal techniques and their potential application, assign extracts to groups of 3 or 4 and nominate one or more characters they should 'prepare to play' (or let groups choose their own).

Ask each group to do the following:

- Work out what the challenges are for the actor playing a particular role in the given extract
- Decide on **two** different rehearsal techniques which they think would be helpful for the actor (ideally focussing on two different challenges)
- Plan how to use the rehearsal technique
- Try it out!

Once groups have tried both rehearsal techniques, they should discuss as a group which technique was most effective and why. If groups are tackling more than one character, repeat the exercise, then all groups should feed back to the whole class.

Preparing to write about rehearsal techniques

In order to avoid vague responses, summarising the approach as follows is helpful:

- What are the challenges for an actor playing x role in y extract?
- Which rehearsal technique would help and why?
- Specifically, how would the technique be used?
- How would the outcome/findings be applied in rehearsal?

Ask students to use their experiences of the 'Rehearsal techniques in action' task to write brief notes for one or both rehearsal techniques.

Eg *Extract: p11-13 (Section 1: Introducing Dan); Fiona; hot-seating*

1. *Challenges = change in mood; show she's happy discussing Dan*
2. *RT = hot-seating; develop understanding of Fiona's positive memories; convey she is happy too*
3. *Light-hearted qus (funny things, D being naughty, etc)*
4. *Use tone, fac/exp, BL when telling hair dye story*

Tackling a rehearsal techniques response

Using the notes from 'Preparing to write about rehearsal techniques', develop them into a response to a 4-mark question about using rehearsal techniques to prepare to play a role. These can be marked by the teacher, or peer-marked* using a generic mark scheme (see past papers/mark schemes on the Eduqas website for specific details, or simply look for answers to the four questions given in the task above).

Eg An actor playing Fiona in this extract has to communicate a happy memory of Dan and show that Fiona enjoys talking about him, after a sombre opening to the play. I would use hot-seating in rehearsal to help the actor to capture this change in mood, focusing on light-hearted questions, such as 'What did Dan do which made you laugh?' and 'What was the naughtiest thing he did when he was little?'. The actor could then draw on the tone of voice, facial expressions and more relaxed body language they used when delivering lines about the hair dye, for example.

* An approach to peer-marking is outlined in Revision.

Timed response to a rehearsal techniques question

Once students have experience of writing about techniques they have actually used and are more confident, set an exam-style question (initially on a scene/character with which they are familiar). Give a time limit (see Top Tip) or, for an early attempt at a timed response, err on the side of generosity. If you want to add more challenge, ask students to use a rehearsal technique they haven't previously tried out/written about.

LEARNING CHECKLIST

✓ Revisit rehearsal techniques, clarifying definition and purpose of each
✓ Explore specific rehearsal techniques relative to a nominated extract/character
✓ Record practical experimentation in preparation for writing a response
✓ Complete an exam-style question

Performance

RESOURCES

- Images of emojis
- Internet access
- *The Laramie Project* (film)
- Theatrefolk website
- Hoodies

Facial expression emojis

This task helps students to avoid vague or unhelpful descriptions of facial expressions (*'They should have an angry face'*; *'I would scrunch my face up'*). Issue pairs with two or three images of emojis and ask them to do the following for each:

- Try to describe the emotion in one word (eg quizzical, impatient, contented)
- Write a brief description of the expression, focusing particularly on eyes/eyebrows and mouth
  - They should write as if answering the question 'how should an actor playing x role use facial expression on y line?'
  - To avoid giving the game away, they must leave out the start of the answer which might say 'To show x is feeling both shock and guilt...' and ensure they don't reference the emotion in their description (eg by saying: the actor's mouth should be downturned sadly, with eyebrows raised in shock!)
  - A good description might read: the actor should have a slightly downturned mouth, with wide eyes and eyebrows raised
- When they have completed their descriptions, they should join up with another pair (keeping the emojis hidden), and see if the new pair can replicate the expressions from the written descriptions alone
- As a four, they can look at any potential improvements needed to clarify or better explain the facial expression required

Playing being 'high' – 1

One thing students should definitely avoid when either performing a scene at the rave, or describing how an actor should perform, is a stereotypical idea of what being 'high' looks like on stage. Ask students to research the effects of MDMA – both those considered 'positive' and side effects, such as those experienced by Dan.

Playing being 'high' – 2

Drawing on the research in task 1, above, use practical exploration to find movements which convey being 'high' clearly to the audience, but which are more suited to the style of the production than simply copying footage from YouTube naturalistically.

- Ask groups to find simple, stylised movements, then experiment with:
  - ○ Exaggeration
  - ○ Synchronisation
  - ○ Pace (slow-motion, extending part of a movement then 'snapping' back to the original pace, etc)

Don't stand in a line!

Look at Chapter 5, where Mark Wheeller talks about static verbatim theatre productions* which seemingly forget the 'theatre' in 'verbatim theatre'. How do you stop *ILYM* being an 'overheard group discussion' – especially Act One, with its Q&A format?

Look at a couple of clips from the film of *The Laramie Project* (a verbatim play about the death of Matthew Shepard in Wyoming in 1998; the film version is on YouTube in full – https://youtu.be/u1qiTmF0p4A) and consider how the actors and director make the interviews dramatically engaging for the audience, for example through: music, juxtaposition of interviews, visual images accompanying the monologues, character choices, setting, etc. How might some of these ideas be employed in *ILYM*?

* This is also discussed in *Verbatim: The Fun of Making Theatre Seriously*, at the end of Chapter 15.

Time-travelling*

One of the challenges of *ILYM* is going seamlessly, but clearly, between interview (present) and flashback (past). 'Time-travelling' uses the verbatim pieces previously produced to explore this idea. It gets students thinking about bringing to life a play which moves back and forth between narrative and flashback, as well as exploring different perspectives. If the pairs introduced lies into their original pieces, they might also consider the impact the telling of the story/other character's responses had on the audience.

If you are not going straight from the initial task into this one, ask pairs to re-cap their work (the 30-second version, or a section around the same length, if they did a longer piece) of their 'what happened yesterday' accounts (the final task, which used both performers playing a single character), then they should develop the work as follows:

- One of the performers narrates the story as a second character who was present/nearby, whilst the other recreates the events through mime, eg:

  A (Mum): Jay is never up early, so yesterday was an exception. It must have been 5.15am *(B (Jay) gets up)* when he headed out of his room *(B carefully opens bedroom door and heads downstairs, reacting to the stairs creaking).*

- Work on a final version of the story in which <u>both</u> A and B narrate and <u>both</u> participate in the flashback (with at least two switches between present and past). At this point the two characters can interact with each other, perhaps to respond, interject or dispute what is said, eg:

  A: Jay is never up early, so yesterday was an exception.
  B: *(rolls his eyes)* Ha ha. *(to audience)* Yes, I woke up early.

A: It must have been 5.15am when he headed out of his room.

B: How did you know what time it was?

A: *(looks at him and shakes head)* I wonder…

B: *(gets up, carefully opens bedroom door and heads downstairs, reacting to the stairs creaking with intakes of breath, etc)*

A: *(sits up in bed, exaggerated sigh)* No need to be quiet – it's not like I was asleep or anything.

B: *(at the bottom of the stairs)* Sandwich time!

A: The kitchen door opened, followed immediately by the fridge. *(looks meaningfully at Jay)* For a change.

B: Fair point.

To reflect on the piece created, the pair should discuss a couple of strong moments, where they clearly conveyed whether it was a flashback or present-tense narration. If they feel none of it was particularly strong, they should discuss how a moment could have been improved or developed.

* This is an extension of the 'Introduction to verbatim' task in Genre & Style

Beginning to write about key moments

The 'Time-travelling' task can be developed into a brief written response which prepares students to write about staging key moments. If they can, instead of saying what they <u>did</u> (eg *'When my mum said that me getting up early was 'an exception', I tutted and said 'ha ha' in a sarcastic tone'* to show she constantly nags me about getting up*), encourage students to change it into instructions explaining what the actors <u>could do</u> (eg *'When the mum tells her son that getting up early is 'an exception', the actor playing the son could tut and say 'ha ha' in a sarcastic tone. This would convey that the son is fed up with her nagging him about getting up'*).

Same lines, different meanings

This is a good way in to exploring vocal techniques, written by Kerry Hinshon and published on the Theatrefolk website (www.theatrefolk.com/blog/19758-2). It explores vocal delivery, allows re-cap of relevant terminology and encourages practical experimentation. The website gives full instructions, but the activity asks students to take a line from the text (I would suggest Alice's line about Dan vomiting on her on p13; George's penultimate line on p30 about not knowing anything; or George's final line about Jack on p31), and work through tasks on the following:

- Emphasis
- Emotion/tone
- 'Sliding scale variations' (exploring range of emotions)

You could extend the task further by looking at other vocal techniques, such as volume, pitch, pace/tempo, pause, intonation.

Alternatively, you could ask students to look at a short speech from the play (such as Megan's speech on p9 – potentially stopping after she quotes Dan, or before she mentions that Monday morning):

- Can students select two or three different ways to deliver the opening paragraph – eg sadly recalling what Dan was like; happy to talk about him again; almost insistent, ensuring Mark really understands what he was like – and experiment with these?
- How can they communicate each approach through altering tone, pace, pitch, emphasis and intonation?
- How did changing these elements alter other aspects of their delivery, such as facial expression, physicality or gesture?
- Can they identify where Megan's emotion changes in the speech? Vocally, how might that contrast be conveyed to the audience?

- They should work to produce their 'definitive' version, which only needs to be performed by one of the pair, the other directing, then show them to the class

Once all versions have been shown, read this from Mark Wheeller's introduction to *Hard To Swallow* (which is equally true of *ILYM*): "The actors should avoid overstatement and should veer towards underplaying [or at least] please avoid any sense of melodrama. You can trust the material... you really can. It is, after all, as close as possible to the real thing".

- As a piece of verbatim theatre, what were the strengths of elements of the performances of Megan's speech?
- Are there any areas where small changes might elicit a more 'truthful' or less 'acted' performance?

Writing about voice

The task above translates really well into an early written vocal response. Using some or all of Megan's speech on p9, ask students to respond to a 4-mark question asking them to explain how vocal skills could be used to convey Megan's character. Either nominate a couple of vocal skills on which they should focus (tone and tempo/pace; volume and emphasis, for example), or ask them to reference at least 2 different vocal techniques.

Add a time limit for greater challenge/exam practice.

Symbolism through action

Look at p25 (*ILYM*, Section 3), just after the repeat of the rave sequence, where the stage directions ask for action to be used to symbolise Dan struggling to stay alive. Ask groups to work on this section and develop a sequence which achieves Mark Wheeller's intentions (ideally, each group would have a hoodie for 'Dan' to wear, which can then be taken from him). They should conclude their sequence with Dan's exit and Jenna remaining on stage, looking at the hoodie.

The Ensemble

How would you want to use the ensemble in *ILYM*? Would you want them on stage all the time? Are there moments when you want 'sparseness' and fewer people on stage? What are those moments and why? Is there the opportunity to use the ensemble as a chorus?, to re-enact events?, to create body props?, through physical theatre? How and when could you employ the ensemble in *IPIWD*, which has a much smaller cast?

LEARNING CHECKLIST

✓ Describe facial expressions precisely
✓ Research and explore conveying the effects of MDMA stylistically
✓ Consider creative approaches to staging verbatim work
✓ Explore moving between interview/narration and flashback
✓ Experiment with vocal techniques, physicality and movement
✓ Consider the role and potential of the ensemble
✓ Translate practical exploration into exam-focused responses

Playing A Role

> **TOP TIP**
>
> In responses, each point should include:
>
> - **When** was/is the line/moment?
> - **What** did/would you do?
> - **How** did/would you do it?
> - **Why** was it done that way?
> - What was/is the intended **effect**?

What's my motivation?

In acting questions focusing on how a role might be played, as well as being asked to consider performance skills – voice, movement and interaction – students are likely to need to discuss motivation. Although a character's motivation will influence every decision the actor makes about how to use performance skills, it is an aspect which students sometimes find challenging to write about. It is worth returning to the character sheets* to discuss the overlap between a character objective and their motivation (and it is helpful to reiterate the distinction between a character's objective/motivation and an actor's, so students do not confuse the two).

In *ILYM*, character motivation is a little complex to discuss, given that the characters in the present, explaining events, have very different motivations from those in the past, recreating them. Ask students to look at a section of the play (the opening of *IPIWD*, Section 5, p55-56 works well) and notice how a character's motivation differs when they are recounting the event many months on, compared to that in the flashback when they are 'in the moment':

- At the start of the section, Tim's motivation is to communicate how 'normal' that night was initially, and how insignificant the 'party' seemed
- He also wants to convey that his initial response to the banging on the door was anger – a typical parental response
- Once he tells the audience it was the police at the door, Tim's motivation is to convey his panic
- As the scene moves into flashback, with Tim questioning the police officer, his motivation is to establish quickly that his son is OK

In small groups, ask students to identify a short extract (1-2 pages) containing both interview and flashback and a character who appears in most of it, and to look at how their motivation differs and changes depending on the context.

* see 'Getting to know the characters' in Characters.

Experimenting with acting techniques

Take a short section of the play (for example, the opening of *IPIWD*, Section 3, p47, where Archie and Kate recall her collecting him from the train station). Choose two physical aspects on which to focus (such as stance, posture, body language, gesture, action, gait, movement, eye contact, facial expression, interaction, positioning on stage) – for example, positioning on stage and movement. Ask groups to work on the section (ideally with a couple more students than the number of actors required), experimenting with the two aspects, making decisions and discussing their justifications for each, focusing on When, What, How, Why, Effect (see Top Tip).

If you wanted to develop this task to include rehearsal techniques, you could ask groups to try using forum theatre as they work, or to address the physical focus of the question by removing the dialogue completely and using mime to see the impact this has.

Short answer acting questions*

Ask students to use what they learned from the task above as the basis for a practice short answer question on how the actors could use positioning on stage and movement to convey their relationship. Remind them to use When, What, How, Why, Effect in their response.

*See also the follow-up task below.

Identifying the When, What, How, Why, Effect

It is very easy to be drawn into vague responses, leaving out the reasons for decisions (or assuming they're obvious!), not being specific about exactly what the actors could do and how, or throwing in the correct terminology without explaining clearly. It is also easy to drift off to cover elements not required.

Eg *The actors should use proxemics to show the distance between them. Archie is reluctant to cross, so he should show this in his face and body language. Kate is pleased Archie is home, so the actor's movements should reflect this, and she should use a relieved tone of voice.*

Before submission or peer or self-marking, ask students to go through their responses with highlighters or different coloured pens. Using a different colour for each of When, What, How, Why, Effect, they should go through their response, highlighting/underlining where these have been covered, and see where the gaps are. In the example above, highlighting would reveal there is no specific What or How; Why is more implied than stated; the intended Effect is mentioned, but not explained; and some of the content is not relevant to the question.

This technique works equally well for 15-mark questions (the longest), although it will save time (and highlighters!) if just one or two paragraphs are targeted.

The same technique can be employed after marking responses: ask students to focus on the weakest paragraph, then use what they have learned from the highlighting/ underlining to improve their responses.

Eg *At the start of the section, the actors could be positioned stage left and stage right, the proxemics reinforcing the distance between them, both emotional and physical. When Archie talks about the ramp between them, the actor could communicate his reluctance to cross and hear the bad news by making eye contact with Kate, lowering his head, suggesting he is avoiding her, then taking a deep breath in and straightening up, as if steeling himself to be there for her, then cross slowly towards Kate, building the tension for the audience. Kate is relieved to have Archie home to support her and Jenna, so the actor should visibly relax when she sees him, dropping her shoulders, exhaling deeply, smiling and lifting her hand in a small wave.*

LEARNING CHECKLIST

- ✓ Understand and identify character motivation
- ✓ Explore physical performance techniques
- ✓ Develop focused written responses
- ✓ Evaluate individual success in meeting exam criteria

Design

Designing a book cover/poster

I am not generally a fan of tasks which seem to be little more than glorified 'colouring in', but I make an except for this one. The process of distilling a play into one image can be really helpful in answering the question 'what is it about?'. If you know what you think a play is 'about', that can be the starting point or the concept you keep returning to in your approach to all design elements.

Ask students to use the work they have completed on Themes, and their own ideas, to decide what is central to the play, and/or the main message they want to communicate to the audience. Once they have this idea they should produce:

- A cover for a new edition of the play, or
- A poster to advertise a production of the play

Besides the obvious information to include, they should give careful thought to:

- Visual impact
- Potential audience/reader response
- Imagery
- Colour
- Style
- Font(s)
- Scale

You could add an element of fun/competition by allowing students to vote for the best designs. To make it a little fairer on the artistically-challenged, have two categories: 'most attractive design' and 'best concept'.

From cover/poster to production design

Which concepts from the designs created are most effective and why? Which visual elements convey meaning most effectively? Which colours would translate well to the stage and why?

How could these visual elements be incorporated into a stage design:

- Through projection?
- A floor cloth?
- Backdrop(s)?
- Items on stage?
- Props?
- Lighting effects?

Students should add the best ideas to their ongoing design notes for reference as they continue to develop their approaches.

Design first

This makes for an interesting group task, with ideas pooled at the end.

- Instead of starting with a section or extract and adding sound, lighting, props, etc, to it, think about it the other way round. Ask some groups to start with a piece of music (one found through the 'Sourcing rave and other music' task in Sound, for example): which scene would it suit? How would they build the scene from there with other design elements?
- Ask other groups to begin with a lighting effect (possibly one found when experimenting with Matt Kizer's 'Labs' in the Lighting, Sound & Projection section): how could music enhance the effect of the lighting? Where might this work in the play?

LEARNING CHECKLIST

✓ Connect 'what is the play about?' to design concepts
✓ Consider and explore elements of stage design
✓ Use sound/lighting as a starting point for creating ideas

Set Design

RESOURCES

- OYT production of *ILYM*
- Settings summaries

Original staging

In the exam, students will need to make reference to the staging of the play in the original production. Sources of information include:

- Richard Long's (set design) and Danny Sturrock's (lighting & multi-media) descriptions of the original designs in Chapters 9 and 10
- The OYT DVD, where the final designs can be seen on stage

Using this information, it is really helpful for students to draw up their own ground plan of the original production, labelled to include as much information as possible on scale, colour, materials, etc. The stage configuration used must also be noted.

Look, too, at the descriptions in Chapter 9 of the light-up cubes used in the original production, particularly their multi-functional role in the design and how the colour-change facility was utilised to create mood and atmosphere.

Stage configurations – pros and cons

Students need to be familiar with the main stage configurations (they may be asked to explain their designs for a specific configuration). There is a helpful summary in the Guidance For Teaching on the Eduqas website, or ask students to use BBC Bitesize (see Top Tip) to research these (potentially as homework preceding a lesson in which the next task is tackled), producing a bullet-point list of pros and cons.

Interestingly, Mark Wheeller has said that if he was staging the production again, he'd consider using a different stage configuration for *IPIWD*. Why might that be? Which two stage configurations would best convey the difference in the two acts?

Linking stage configuration to design response

Knowing the limitations of a stage configuration obviously allows students to avoid the main pitfalls when designing their set (such as staging flats in the middle of a traverse stage), but if they also know the positives, they can discuss how they will exploit them through their design. Ask students to produce starter sentences for a general design question in which each of the main stage configurations is specified:

Eg *Having a theatre-in-the-round stage configuration would enable me to…*

Eg *Staging the play end-on would give me the flexibility to…*

131

Expanding the settings summary

If they completed them, students can use the settings summary (see Structure) to start considering the locations they need and would like to create. How frequently is each location used? How important are they to the play as a whole? What is the best way to indicate location – through set, projection, lighting, props, costume? How can they make their set design flexible and adaptable to work with the frequent changes in location? How might they exploit elements such as colour, levels, materials and scale?

If they have a saved copy of the summary as a table, students could add a column for their notes on settings or use the blank column on their paper copy. These can then be referenced as a starting point for their set designs.

Symbolic elements

In Chapter 8, Alysha-Jade Patis mentions working with Tim Ford in a rehearsal, and his idea (not ultimately used, but giving rise to another) to scatter the stage with water bottles, the cast moving around them. There are parallels between this and The Paper Birds' verbatim production of *Thirsty*, with glasses of water lined up downstage, serving both a symbolic and a practical purpose in the play.

The Paper Birds are keen that every element of their sets is used in performance, with nothing serving solely as 'set-dressing'. Applying this idea to *ILYM*, what key, usable items might form part of the set design? What is the message being communicated to the audience by using particular props or items in this way?

LEARNING CHECKLIST

✓ Identify the key features of the original production
✓ Evaluate different stage configurations and their impact on design
✓ Explore locations in the play and begin to develop design concepts for these
✓ Consider the potential for symbolism in design

Props

TOP TIP

In exam questions, props and set design are often combined. Eduqas defines props as "furnishings, set dressings, and all items, large and small, which cannot be classified as scenery, electrics or wardrobe"; hand props are those handled by actors; personal props are kept in an actor's costume

RESOURCES

- Hoodies
- Water bottles

Key Props*

When Mark Wheeller was developing the first production of *Race To Be Seen* (previously known by its subtitle *Graham: The World's Fastest Blind Runner*), he suggested the cast have no props or scenery other than a white stick for every cast member. If this idea was applied to *ILYM*, what one prop would you give each cast member, or a particular group, such as Dan's family or friends? How might these props be imaginatively used?

In one production of *ILYM* which Mark saw, hula-hoops were employed very effectively by the cast. How might these be used in the 'rave' sequence to create an appropriate atmosphere?

* Also consider set elements as props (see 'Symbolic elements' in Set Design).

The Hoodie*

The Hoodie (see also Costume), worn by members of the ensemble playing Dan, doubles as both costume and prop. It is described in the opening stage directions as being lovingly taken care of throughout the play by Jenna, who delivers it to the member of the ensemble playing Dan. How might the actor playing Jenna use this prop? Are there moments where she sets it down? Where and how? When and how might the audience's focus be taken back to the hoodie?

Look at the key moments where the hoodie becomes a significant and symbolic prop in the play:

- p13, the hoodie is returned to Jenna
- p25, Jenna is unable to get it back
- p25, Dan (Ensemble 4) lays the hoodie down, exits and Jenna looks back at it
- p28, Jenna picks up the hoodie and exits cradling it
- p39, at the start of *IPIWD*, the hoodie is described as hanging on the hat stand
- p57, the only time Fiona takes the hoodie (prop) and puts it on Ensemble 4 as Dan (costume)
- p62, the hoodie is returned to the hat stand, and Fiona lovingly touches it

What is the added significance of the prop given that it isn't just something 'belonging to Dan', but actually represents him and distinguishes those playing him?

In the one-act TIE production by Stopwatch Theatre Company/Wizard Theatre, they used the hoodie as a 'puppet', members of the cast manipulating it to represent Dan. Take a short extract (Section 3, p20-21, the texted dialogue between Alice and Dan, works well) and either have groups of 4/5, or use forum theatre with a group of volunteers. Ask the students to try out the scene – two or possibly three manipulating the hoodie, one actor reading Dan/Ensemble 3's line, and the other reading Alice's lines. Can they add a prop phone and make it look like 'Dan' is texting?

What was the impact of using the hoodie to denote Dan? How might this work throughout the play, rather than the hoodie going from symbolic prop to identifying costume item as OYT used it? What might be the challenges or limitations of this approach?

* see Chapter 12 for detailed discussion of how the hoodie came to be such a key item in the play.

Water bottles

In the original OYT production of *ILYM*, another key prop – the water bottles – emerged from a different idea*. In Chapter 8, Sally Britton (Hope in the OYT production) and Carley Sefton Wilson (Assistant Director of OYT) discuss the significance of this prop and the origins of the decision to light them up, Dan's in red to signify the dangerously high dose of MDMA he is about to take (as illustrated on the cover of this book). What connections can students see between the choice of water bottles and the text/subject matter?

In Chapter 10, Danny Sturrock talks about the use of water bottles in the original production. If they were used in a production, how might they be employed beyond the rave scene? Select a brief extract (if you want to add more challenge, choose one where the water bottles seem particularly incongruous or unhelpful!) and ask students to experiment, in groups, with using them, besides for their intended purpose. Each group should select their two best ideas to share with the class.

* see Set Design – Symbolic elements.

Writing a props response

Basing their responses on the task above, and using any of the ideas they or others came up with, students write a response to a question about how props might be used in the given extract to create meaning. This could be a brief 4-mark question, asking for two uses of a prop, with explanation of the choices, or a 6-mark question, with 1 mark for the use of the prop, and 2 for the justification/link to the text.

LEARNING CHECKLIST

✓   Identify and consider key props
✓   Explore, practically, how specific props might be used in performance
✓   Complete an exam-style question

Costume, Hair & Make-up

Costume design

Look at Chapter 13, and particularly Kat Chiver's costume design concept and her guiding principle for *ILYM* that she didn't want "flashy costumes". Why might this be the case for *ILYM*, in particular? Kat also states that she didn't want any costume changes. What might be the connection between this decision and the play's structure?

Assign a different character to each individual (or let them choose); you may well have some duplication, which is not a bad thing. The hoodie is the only costume referenced in the play, so Mark Wheeller has given those staging the play a lot of freedom in terms of costume design. Students should consider the information on costume outlined above and design a costume (this makes a good homework task), on one side of A4 (to keep it concise and aid scanning/copying) and in colour (for obvious reasons). The design can be hand-drawn, a computer graphic, or use images from the internet (or cut out of magazines, if they want to go old-school!) to illustrate the various items of clothing they select. Each item should be annotated with notes to illustrate why it has been chosen. Throughout the work the following should be covered:

- Period
- Style
- Garment
- Fit
- Fabric
- Colour
- Reasons for choice connected to character

A range of good examples covering the various groups (friends, family, ensemble) can be scanned and made available to the class, or copied/displayed to use as reference.

Base costume

Although it is possible the family will be dressed to distinguish them from the rest of the cast (see the task 'Differentiating between the different groups' below), most of the ensemble will probably need a base costume. It can be tempting to state that the ensemble should 'wear all black', with no further details; decisions still need to be made for the bullet points in the task above, and the description needs to be clear, with every aspect covered (see Top Tip). This can be recorded similarly to the costume task above (as a visual, annotated image), or as a brief written description.

In addition, students may choose to use a 'suggestion of costume' to distinguish other, minor characters, such as the Police or First Aiders. Drawing up a list of these characters and deciding on a clearly identifying item for each (eg an item of clothing or a hat), then adding these details to the image/description of the base costume, is well worth doing.

The hoodie

As discussed in Props, the hoodie has significance beyond an item of costume. Consider the added meaning the hoodie has and how the wearing of it by members of the ensemble might impact the audience differently because of this. As the costume designer, from a practical perspective, what are the considerations when sourcing the hoodie? What decisions would they make? In pairs or small groups, students should draw up a list of these, considering the bullet-point list in the costume design task above, then feed back and discuss their observations and choices. Some of these might include:

- Period: modern, although hoodies have barely changed since the 70s; helpfully 'timeless' item
- Style: needs to be full-zip for ease/speed of changes; a recognisable brand creates connotations (which may sway the audience's perception of Dan); may be best avoided by having no logo/brand name
- Fit: must fit largest ensemble member playing Dan; sufficiently roomy to make changes easy
- Colour: needs to stand out when hoodie is a prop; also differentiate Dan from other characters when worn by ensemble; what are symbolic associations for different colours?
- Fabric: likely to be jersey; specifying lightweight cotton jersey ensures it is easy to perform in/hard-wearing
- Condition: Dan's social class and background means it is unlikely to be threadbare; should be 'worn-in' – association of being favourite item of Dan's

Another aspect to consider is what the ensemble is wearing as a base costume. If they wear long sleeves (such as a long-sleeved t-shirt), it will be harder and slower to get in and out of the hoodie than if they wear a t-shirt and have bare arms.

Although this might seem like an extreme amount of detail for one item of costume, it is a good example through which to increase students' awareness of the many elements a costume designer must consider. Thinking in this depth and detail avoids the kind of costume responses where actors are required to negotiate multi-level sets in maxi-dresses; middle-aged, middle-class mothers are dressed in short skirts; or a cast is expected to do a high-energy performance wearing several layers topped off with puffer jackets.

Differentiating between the different groups

How might costume be used to distinguish between the friends and the family? Is there any value in differentiating those at the rave with Dan from his other friends? Would you want Mark to stand out in some way or to appear 'other'?

Writing a costume response

Basing their responses on costume design ideas developed so far – theirs and/or others' – students produce a response to a question asking for their costume design for a nominated (or chosen) character. Ask students to consider how costume communicates the character to the audience and give aspects on which they should focus (eg garments, colour, fit, condition). A 6-mark question allows scope for a helpfully detailed response.

LEARNING CHECKLIST

- ✓ Consider costume design alongside the subject matter and atmosphere of the play
- ✓ Explore detail required in making costume design decisions
- ✓ Develop individual costume designs
- ✓ Complete an exam-style question

Sound, Lighting & Projection

RESOURCES

- Internet access (YouTube, Spotify, etc)
- OYT production of *ILYM*
- TiE It Up! production of *ILYM*
- Matt Kizer's website: scenicandlighting.com
- BBC interview with Fiona and Tim
- Bank of headlines, images, etc, from the 'Social, historical & cultural context' task

Sourcing rave and other music

Ask students to research rave music and find tracks to be shared with the rest of the class which might work for the rave sequences. Assigning slightly different genres to individuals or groups – for example, techno, house, trance

– should result in a greater variety of tracks and ensure everyone doesn't come in armed with the same 'Top Ten Rave Tracks'!

Are there tracks or sections of tracks which would work as underscoring in other scenes in the play? Would any effectively punctuate moments or enhance transitions between scenes?

Soundscaping/sound effects/soundtracking

Sometimes, sound in theatre is thought of as boiling down to sound effects and music. As with props, it can be tempting – particularly for the less technically-minded students – to see sound as something which is just 'added' to a performance, rather than something which is integral to it and <u>designed</u>. Encourage a creative approach by asking students to develop a sound <u>design</u>, rather than thinking about simply adding sound effects and music.

Re-cap or introduce these components of sound design:

- Soundscapes* (creating a sense of place or a mood or atmosphere through sound, but without words or dialogue)
- Sound effects* (live/practical or pre-recorded/canned)
- Underscoring
- Diegetic (heard by the characters)
- Non-diegetic (having an external source)

In addition, I like the concept of 'soundtracking' (as described by Jonothan Neelands in *Structuring Drama Work*), which is essentially layering or combining any or all of the above to give a sense of place, create a mood or atmosphere, and/or accompany an action.

Choose an extract from the play and ask groups to experiment, source, design and potentially perform or record the sound for it. Depending on time available and the expertise of the students, you might also ask them to consider levels, source, direction, style, key, etc. If you have both, watch the same scene in the OYT and TiE It Up! productions of *ILYM* on video, and compare the different choices made in sound design.

* A really clear way of highlighting just how much can be created by the human voice, and how effectively the ensemble might be used in this regard, is to play students a sound-effect track such as 'Street Ambience Sound Effect' (https://youtu.be/F6S77At4Qvk) and Aaron Schumacher's 'Life On The Street' (https://youtu.be/9u1USzmj3ZA), an all-vocal soundscape.

Lighting design in the original production

In the exam, lighting may be a question on its own or linked to other design elements (such as sound or set design, or as part of a more general 'visual elements' question). Clearly, it makes little sense to discuss lighting in isolation, as illustrated by the design decisions made by Danny Sturrock (Lighting & Multimedia Design), discussed in Chapter 10. Look at what he says about the illuminated water bottles and light-up cubes and what he felt was the main purpose of any additional lighting. Also read what he says about the simplicity of the lighting design, the few exceptions and how backlight was used, and why 'less is more'.

Watch brief extracts from the OYT performance, tying Danny's description to what can be seen on stage. What is the effect of the backlit blue wash in key scenes? Can students identify the 'less is more' approach? Is mood and atmosphere successfully created by elements besides lighting?

Lighting: colour, angles, gobos

Matt Kizer has a great website – scenicandlighting.com – which allows students to experiment with colour, intensity, angles and gobos. 'Color Lab', 'Gobo Lab' and 'Dance

Lighting Lab' are all free to use on his website. A really helpful and instructive homework (or lesson task, if you have computer access), is to use one or more of the Labs to design lighting states for a particular scene. Or you can use it in a lesson to demonstrate how angles, intensity, colour, etc, could be altered subtly to create a different mood or atmosphere at particular points in the play.

Developing lighting design ideas

For the following task, you could either put these questions to the group for discussion, ask small groups to discuss them and feed back, or set it as an individual, written task to be completed at home.

Select or assign a section or short extract (for example, *IPIWD*, Section 4). If students were designing the lighting for a production of *ILYM* which did not make use of illuminated bottles or light-up cubes, how would they respond to these questions:

- How could lighting contribute to the set design?
- How might lighting convey time of day, location, interior/exterior setting, mood/atmosphere?
- How might colour and intensity be used?
- How could focus be created to direct the audience's attention?
- Which lanterns might achieve the best effects in which scenes/sections?
- How might particular effects be used to highlight specific moments?
- Do you want lighting to reflect the style of the section – eg some scenes more naturalistic, others stylised?
- Where might lighting need to alter – to convey a change in mood, for example?

Elements/terminology they may consider include: lanterns, angle, wash, spotlight, intensity, diffusion, colour, cool, warm, gel, LED, gobo, specials, strobe, haze.

Projection of photos/film of Dan

What is the purpose and potential impact on the audience of using real pictures of Dan, as described in the stage directions? What would the impact be if the photos were 'recreated' by members of the cast, perhaps with the hoodie used prominently to tie them to 'Dan' in the play? Or if 'generic' images of children were used, possibly intentionally diverse in ethnicity and gender?

There is only one use of video in the stage directions: on p14 a video of Dan playing guitar and singing with Hope is referenced. How do students think a video might differ in impact? What about at this particular point in the play?

Clips of this video form part of a BBC interview* with Fiona and Tim, six months after Dan's death. It is worth showing the BBC piece, particularly as the video is juxtaposed with spoken memories of Dan – just as it is in the play. What are the students' feelings on its potential impact in performance, having seen it?

Finally, look at Danny Sturrock's description of how the ideas evolved from the starting point of using projection-mapping (Chapter 10). Where should the projections go? Onto the set? A cyclorama? Projection screens? How can use of projection be adapted for stage configurations such as theatre-in-the-round or traverse?

* The interview is one of a number of videos on the *I Love You, Mum – I Promise I Won't Die* playlist on Mark Wheeller's YouTube channel, which is a really helpful resource.

Developing use of projection – 1

Ask students to consider further ways in which projection could be used in a production of *ILYM*, for example:

- To establish location and time/date
- To emphasise a theme or issue

- To create mood or atmosphere
- To guide or elicit audience response
- To reinforce key moments or dialogue

A useful reference here is the film of *The Laramie Project*. It is worth showing the class at least one clip (for example the 'media circus' scene from 26:26 – 28:34) to examine how it uses interviews, flashback, voiceover, montage of headlines, images of landmarks, etc, and news footage – real and re-created. Although it is a film version of the play, the way in which these elements are layered makes for some interesting comparisons with the role multi-media played in the original production of *ILYM*, and the potential to take a similar approach when staging *ILYM*. It is also interesting to compare the beginning of the clip mentioned with how Act 2 (*IPIWD*) begins, with the press conference. In the film, how are music, colour, actor responses, contrasts in movement and stillness used to create a strong theatrical moment?

Developing use of projection – 2

Students may well already have a bank of newspaper headlines, images, etc, from the 'Social, historical & cultural context' task in Themes & Issues. If not, ask individuals or groups to source those on Dan's story, similar cases, trial reports and articles on drugs – potentially as a homework task ahead of the lesson. How might these be used in a production of *ILYM*?

- In a projected montage before the play begins?
- Between sections?
- At key points in the play?

Ask students to identify particular images and points where they might be used. How will they be projected – one large image, in black and white, as a montage, etc?

Developing use of projection – 3

Finally, ask students to take on the role of 'projection designer' to consider the question: how might the use of projection reflect an overall message?

The brief: the director has chosen to focus on these words on the DSM Foundation website: "if this could happen to someone like Dan, it could happen to anyone". In small groups, students should produce a short presentation to be given to the director, outlining their vision for the use of projection in *ILYM*. They will need to outline (with visual examples, if resources allow):

- How they envisage projections being shown on stage (eg onto a cyc, scenery, etc)
- How projection will bookend the play
- At least three points in the play (other than those mentioned in the stage directions) where projection will play a significant role

Writing about projection

From task 2 or 3 above, students should select one of their chosen key points in the play where projection will play an important role. They should write a response to a 4-mark question asking how projection could be used to convey meaning to the audience at that point in the play. They should consider what they are projecting onto, its positioning on stage, choice of images/footage, scale and colour. They should give reasons for their ideas.

If students are experienced, you could set the question as timed practice.

LEARNING CHECKLIST

- ✓ Explore potential uses/sources of sound in performance
- ✓ Compare use of sound and lighting in productions of *ILYM*, including the original production
- ✓ Explore elements of lighting using computer applications
- ✓ Explore the role and potential of projection
- ✓ Develop individual sound, lighting and projection design ideas
- ✓ Complete an exam-style question

TOP TIP

When tackling an extract, consider:

- What are the 5-8 key moments?
- What is the mood/atmosphere I want to create?
- How is that best achieved?
- How do I want the audience to respond?
- How can I achieve this through acting/design?

RESOURCES

- OYT production of *ILYM*
- TiE It Up! production of *ILYM*
- Tracks from 'Sourcing rave and other music' task
- 'Children' (dream version) by Robert Miles
- Instructions & music for Frantic Assembly's 'Quad'

Directing an extract

This task is best started in one lesson, then completed in another one or two. Although it is time-consuming, by the end students will have seen a number of extracts brought to life, and heard design or directorial ideas from everyone in the class. Each group will be involved in two tasks:

1. Plan, design and direct an extract
2. Serve as actors for another group

Task 1 – preparation:

- In groups of 4-7, assign or ask students to select an extract (approximately 1.5-2 pages of text)
- Each person in the group should take on one or two areas of responsibility (directing, lighting, sound, projection, costume, set and props). You may wish to assign, and pre-brief, the directors, as this is the most challenging role in this task
- The designers will need to prepare a brief summary of their decisions, which they will deliver
- The directors will need to prepare for the following: in the delivery part of the task, the director will have 15 minutes to quickly brief the actors about their intentions for the scene, then conduct a 'live rehearsal' with them in front of the rest of the class. Directors may take any approach, but should allow time for a run-through of the scene within the 15 minutes
- Give all groups the same stage configuration to work with (end-on is obviously the most straightforward)
- Allow planning and preparation time (depending on the level of sophistication required, half an hour should be plenty)
- Group members can use the time before the next lesson to prepare feedback for their area of responsibility

Task 2 – preparation:

- Assign each group the extract they will take on as actors
- Either cast roles or allow the group to decide (multi-roling is fine)
- At home, in preparation for the next lesson, the actors should look over the extract briefly, so they are not reading cold (lines do not need to be learnt!)

Delivery – each group taking it in turns:

- The designers begin by outlining their ideas for each design element for the extract
- The director then has 15 minutes in which to brief, rehearse with, and do a run-through of the extract with the actors
- The class should observe and look for:
  - How well the intentions for the extract were achieved by designers and director
  - Favourite design ideas and why
  - Examples of good directing techniques
  - The most effective/powerful moment(s) on stage and why
  - Ideas they liked for interpreting the characters/ extract

Writing about an extract

Develop the task above into a written response, by asking students to write a 6-mark answer to a question about how they would use [nominated design or acting element] to convey the extract effectively to an audience, for one of the following:

- The directing/design area for which they took responsibility, based on their own extract
- Voice and facial expression, or movement and gesture, or use of space and interaction in the role/extract in which they acted
- A nominated design element/role for one of the extracts, chosen by the teacher

Add a time limit (7.5 minutes, based on a-minute-a-mark + 25%) to give students exam practice.

Same scene, different approach

Encourage students to start making evaluative decisions about the effectiveness of different approaches by showing them two or more filmed versions of the same extract (I would use the OYT and TiE It Up! productions). As before, I would hold off until you are confident students have some of their own ideas, but showing two versions – one the amateur, original production, directed by the playwright; the other a professional production – should encourage them to embrace different approaches.

Focus questioning on aspects such as:

- Moments which had the greatest impact and why
- Design elements they found most effective
- Acting techniques which conveyed characters or relationships particularly well
- How space and the movement within it differed in the productions
- Aspects which they think could be developed further or altered in some way
- Ideas they have which spring from seeing one or both versions

KEY SCENE – THE RAVE: *ILYM* Section 1, p7; Section 3, p25

An active way in

This is a simple adaptation of the game 'Captain's Coming'/'Pirates', which you may well have used as 'Upstage/Downstage' (shout a command, students move to a specific area of the stage, strike a pose, etc). For obvious reasons, I call this version 'Rave'. A few suggested commands are given below, but add your own or ask students to suggest some:

'Beat drop' = freeze in a dance pose

- 'Best mate' = grab a partner and both slur 'You're my best mate'
- 'Tune!' = run to the middle and jump up and down
- 'Police are coming!' = run to the edge of the space

The aim isn't to make light of what happened to Dan, but to capture some of the energy of the rave, as it would have been before Dan became ill.

Choosing music

How could music be used in the rave sequence? Is it better to use a widely-recognised track? What is the effect of this? (could seem less threatening; the associations are likely to be more benign)

What is the impact on audience if you use a track which is not instantly recognisable? A track which builds gradually? Something 'darker', with a very strong beat? If it is played uncomfortably loudly?

Look at what Paul Ibbott (Composer and MD for the OYT production) says in Chapter 11 about the role and use of music and underscoring in the play. Return to the tracks found in the 'Sourcing rave and other music' task (see Sound, Lighting & Projection). Which of these could work and why? Do they fulfil the functions Paul describes?

Physicalising the rave

This task could be done completely in smaller groups, but I like the greater impact of doing it mostly as a whole class. It also has the advantage that the students can focus on one track while they work, rather than being distracted by numerous others being played around them!

- Give students a track to work with or allow them to choose one from those they sourced in the earlier task. I like the 'dream version' of 'Children' by Robert

Miles (https://youtu.be/ckiuB3VmHJk) because it builds so gradually (the beat-drop is more than two minutes in) and there are more than seven minutes of material, allowing students to select different sections for the rave sequence, the repeat of the rave, and as underscoring in other scenes

- Begin with a warm-up, such as Frantic Assembly's 'Quad'. The version I learned was from a workshop with the company many years ago, but there is a good description of the general principles here: https://www.curiousonstage.com/content/uploads/2015/01/Jumping-Drama-Exercise.pdf
- Once students have mastered the basics, send each 'line' off as a group to develop movements for 2 or 3 of the beats. These could be 'dance-like' in origin, but the intention is not to create a dance sequence; each move should happen firmly on a beat (or on two half-beats). For example, fist pump with right hand on beat 2; two claps, beginning on the upbeat (the 'and') of '3 and 4'
- Bring groups back and see each line's movements. Incorporate these into the sequence and rehearse
- Now go back to the beginning of the sequence. Do you want the rave to build gradually or to have a more impactful opening? What works best with the track/section of it selected? Try beginning with the whole group bouncing from the very start. Then try a version where each line gets into position 'flashmob' style (initially at the edges, acting naturalistically, then getting into position ready to jump on beat 1), until the whole group is present
- Decide on a cue to complete the Quad sequence. What happens next? Freestyle dancing still in a 'block'? A more naturalistic mix of dancing and other interactions? Try out some different approaches
- What is the cue for the transition into panic? Experiment with techniques such as mime, soundscape, slow-motion, etc

- Would the group alter the sequence when it repeats in Act 2? If so, how? Would they shorten it?

Adding technical/design elements

Unless you have a lot of time and resources, or plenty of design candidates, developing the 'Physicalising the rave' task above further, with ideas for lighting, sound effects, projection, etc, may only be possible through discussion, but it is still well worth doing.

Notes on the rave

Ask students to summarise their rave sequence in note form. They could approach it from an acting perspective, focusing on movement, use of space, physicality, etc, or design, concentrating on music, sound effects, lighting, etc, or they could cover both. Guide them to note the mood or atmosphere they intended to create (and the changes in this), as well as how this was achieved.

Tackling an exam response

You could approach this in a number of ways, but I would recommend setting a longer, higher-tariff question at this stage (15 marks being the highest in the exam):

- Treat it as an acting or design question, or merge the two (which, although unlikely in the exam, is an efficient '2-for-1' approach to practice addressing all aspects of a question); include bullet points outlining what students should cover
- Allow students to refer to their notes as they write or 'revise' from them in advance
- You could introduce an additional layer of complexity by stating the stage configuration they should use
- Possible questions include: 'How would you use the ensemble to stage the rave sequence at the start of

the play?'; 'Describe how you would combine design and performance elements to stage the rave sequence on a traverse stage'; 'Outline your ideas for sound and lighting in the rave sequence'

Add a time limit (length depending on the scope of the question) for additional exam practice.

OTHER KEY SCENES

Use similar approaches to those outlined above for the rave sequence, and/or a range of tasks from throughout the scheme of work, to explore other key scenes, focusing on the challenges and questions specific to that scene. For example:

The Funeral (*IPIWD*, Section 2, p43-45):

- How might the stage space be used to convey the sense of the coffin moving through the streets?
- How could proxemics be used to show the different groups and their connections to each other? Where might the proxemics change to show unity or individual relationships?
- How could sound be used to create a sense of location and atmosphere? What is the role of silence in this extract?
- Does costume need to be different for the funeral, or is this something that needs to be considered when designing the costumes to avoid changes?

The Sycamore Seeds (*ILYM*, Section 1 p7-8; *IPIWD*, Section 7, p63-65)

- The sycamore seeds that Fiona and Tim hold are a strong visual image, but the seeds themselves are small. How could you ensure these 'play' on stage?
- Do they have sufficient symbolic significance to consider including them in the stage design in some way? If so, how?

- The sycamore seeds travelling can be seen as a metaphor for Dan's life. How might this sense of movement be physicalised in the short section from p7 to Mark's speech on p8? And in the longer 'journey' of Dan's life described from p63 to the revealing of the chair on p65?
- How might lighting be used to direct the audience's focus through the longer of these two journeys? Or to create a sense of 'difference' in this final scene?
- The stage directions describe the final, ensemble scene as including the whole cast. What is the role of the ensemble in this scene? How might they be used to create an appropriate atmosphere?

LEARNING CHECKLIST

✓ Draw together students' learning and ideas on all elements to approach an extract
✓ Compare different directorial approaches to the play
✓ Use exemplar scenes to explore design and performance approaches
✓ Translate learning into a high-tariff, exam-style question

Revision

RESOURCES

- Eduqas website
- Mark scheme
- Sample response to high-tariff question

Exam question builder

Asking the class to create their own exam questions has numerous benefits:

- Finding suitable sections/characters/questions provides further opportunities for students to review the text

- Researching and considering potential questions ensures students are prepared for a greater range of questions
- Questions produced by a whole class will be considerably more diverse
- It allows students to produce more practice questions for their own use in revision
- They may provide you with a few more questions you can use with them or future cohorts!

Once students are familiar with the structure of the paper and types of question, they should complete their own research using sample/past papers (those publicly available on the Eduqas website) and begin to write their own questions and mark schemes. Use the 'extract table' you drew up initially to assign extracts (of around 3 pages) to individuals or pairs; any 'spare' extracts can be used as extension tasks.

Depending on the time available, the questions could be: shared with all students; reviewed and issued regularly by you; used as practice questions for the whole class/ individuals wanting/needing additional practice; for discussion in class; to be answered in note form or as a brief plan. They can also be used for additional peer-marking (see 'Peer marking' task below).

Mark schemes

Writing mark schemes can seem laborious and not much fun – especially for students who are inexperienced at such tasks – but it's a really useful exercise for a number of reasons:

- Careful scrutiny of marking criteria develops students' awareness of how marks are awarded
- Writing a mark scheme encourages students to consider a broad approach to answering questions

- It encourages students to focus their own responses towards marking criteria
- It ensures answers are more precisely structured and written to secure potential marks

You could make the task more interesting by handing a question produced in the 'Exam question builder' task (above) to another pair and asking them to produce the mark scheme, then passing the question on to another pair to attempt (individually), and finally the responses and mark scheme to a further pair to mark (each person in the pair marking a response, then swapping to 'double-mark'). The logistics and timings of this will be a little challenging, but it adds a competitive element which students may enjoy.

Peer marking

The first time you do peer-marking with a class, use a short question (of around 4 marks) where marks are very clearly and specifically applied. Re-cap the nature of the question and how marks are awarded (display or hand out the mark scheme). Mitigate potential embarrassment by reminding students how much can be learned from what people get wrong, as well as what they get right. An individual's wrong or incomplete answer encourages the marker to consider what could be changed or added, which is hugely beneficial. It is not a task in which the focus is solely 'getting the answer right'.

- Give students the questions and an appropriate amount of time to complete it (allowing extra time for those who qualify)
- Once completed, students swap, find a colour to mark in and mark, indicating through ticks where good, relevant points have been made. In the margin, they should note the point being rewarded (eg 'tone' to show tone has been correctly referenced). Sum up with a general comment on anything missing/incorrect and

what was good. Give a total mark. (Allow 5 minutes for marking the answer)
- Swap to another student; select a different colour
- Repeat until it has been marked three times, making sure each set of marks is clear
- Return responses and survey how many had three markers agree or very nearly agree
- Discuss where differences of opinion occurred and where marking may not have been accurate (eg marks awarded for good points but not relevant to the question, or where the same point was repeated)
- Take in and check marking, awarding a mark overall. Return so student and markers can see where the response was rewarded/how accurately it was marked

It is worth repeating the exercise in a later lesson with a slightly longer question, or expanding the task to individual marking of a longer, anonymous response (eg a sample, one written by you or from a previous year's cohort.

LEARNING CHECKLIST

✓ Research and compile exam questions
✓ Create specific and detailed mark schemes
✓ Test understanding and application of marking criteria to responses through peer-marking

Resources

I Love You, Mum – I Promise I Won't Die – DVD of original production by Oasis Youth Theatre, SalamanderStreet.com

I Love You, Mum – I Promise I Won't Die – streamed production by TiE It Up! Theatre, tiu-theatre.co.uk

Mark Wheeller YouTube channel – youtube.com/c/MarkWheeller

National Theatre YouTube channel – youtube.com/c/NationalTheatre

Daniel Spargo-Mabbs Foundation – dsmfoundation.org.uk

BBC Bitesize – bbc.co.uk/bitesize

TiE It Up! Theatre – tiu-theatre.co.uk

Matt Kizer: Scenic and Lighting Design – scenicandlighting.com

Theatrefolk – theatrefolk.com

The Curious Incident of the Dog in the Nighttime (NT) – curiousonstage.com

The Laramie Project (film) – written and directed by Moises Kaufman, 2002

Thirsty, The Paper Birds – thepaperbirds.com

Drama Schemes by Mark Wheeller, Rhinegold Education, 2010

Verbatim: The Fun of Making Theatre Seriously by Mark Wheeller, Salamander Street, 2021

Hard To Swallow: Easy To Digest by Mark Wheeller & Karen Latto, PPing Publishing, 2017

Structuring Drama Work by Jonothan Neelands, Cambridge University Press, 1990

The Frantic Assembly Book of Devising Theatre by Scott Graham and Steven Hoggett, Routledge, 2014

I Love You, Mum – I Promise I Won't Die Drama Teacher's Resource Pack – TiE It Up! Theatre

Acknowledgements

I should like to thank the following:

Mark, for commissioning this scheme of work, having faith in me, and providing inspiration and support along the way.

My students, past and present, for their enthusiasm for Mark's plays, for testing out ideas neither they nor I ever expected to be published, and especially those to whom I tentatively mentioned the possibility of writing this scheme of work, who were so touchingly encouraging and excited!

My friends and colleagues in my department, Rachel, Julian and Ed, who gave me the confidence to say yes.

Tony Baxter, the first person with whom I ever directed, and a master of taking a play 'from page to stage'.

My wonderful family, who always show such enormous interest in everything I do, despite theatre not really being their 'thing'.

And finally John, for his unwavering support and belief in me.

Available from Salamander Street

Milton Keynes UK
Ingram Content Group UK Ltd.
UKHW021447150124
436070UK00031B/468

9 781914 228766